SAMS
Teach Yourself

C++

Jesse Liberty

in 10 Minutes

SAMS

A Division of Macmillan Computer Publishing
201 West 103rd St., Indianapolis, Indiana, 46290 USA

SAMS TEACH YOURSELF C++ IN 10 MINUTES

Copyright 1999 by Sams Publishing

International Standard Book Number: 0-672-31603-X

Library of Congress Catalog Card Number: 99-60194

Printed in the United States of America

First Printing: March 1999

01   00   4

TRADEMARKS

WARNING AND DISCLAIMER

EXECUTIVE EDITOR
Tracy Dunkelberger

ACQUISITIONS EDITOR
Holly Allender

DEVELOPMENT EDITOR
Sean Dixon

MANAGING EDITOR
Jodi Jensen

PROJECT EDITOR
Dawn Pearson

COPY EDITOR
Mary Lagu

INDEXER
Mary Gammons

PROOFREADERS
Eddie Lushbaugh
Dawn Pearson

TECHNICAL EDITOR
Donald Xie

TEAM COORDINATOR
Michelle Newcomb

INTERIOR DESIGN
Gary Adair

COVER DESIGN
Aren Howell

LAYOUT TECHNICIANS
Brandon Allen
Stacey DeRome
Timothy Osborn
Staci Somers

TABLE OF CONTENTS

ABOUT THE AUTHOR

Jesse Liberty is president of Liberty Associates, Inc. (http://www.libertyassociates.com), which provides custom, on-site instruction, mentoring, consulting, and contract programming in C++, Java, and object-oriented software development. Jesse has published several books on C++ and object-oriented programming, including *Sams Teach Yourself C++ in 21* Days, *Sams Teach Yourself C++ in 24 Hours*, and *C++ Unleashed*. He also writes a monthly column for *C++ Report*. Jesse has been a software architect for Xerox, a distinguished software engineer for AT&T, and Vice President of Citibank's Development Division. He can be reached at jliberty@libertyassociates.com.

DEDICATION

This book is dedicated to you, faithful reader.

ACKNOWLEDGMENTS

I must first thank my family, who continue to support my writing and to put up with my insane schedule. I also want to thank the folks at Sams, especially Tracy Dunkelberger, Holly Allender, Sean Dixon, Mary Lagu, and Dawn Pearson.

TELL US WHAT YOU THINK!

As the reader of this book, *you* are our most important critic and commentator. We value your opinion and want to know what we're doing right, what we could do better, what areas you'd like to see us publish in, and any other words of wisdom you're willing to pass our way.

As the Executive Editor for the Advanced Programming and Distributed Architectures team at Macmillan Computer Publishing, I welcome your comments. You can fax, email, or write me directly to let me know what you did or didn't like about this book—as well as what we can do to make our books stronger.

Please note that I cannot help you with technical problems related to the topic of this book, and that due to the high volume of mail I receive, I might not be able to reply to every message.

When you write, please be sure to include this book's title and author as well as your name and phone or fax number. I will carefully review your comments and share them with the author and editors who worked on the book.

Fax:	317-817-7070
Email:	programming@mcp.com
Mail:	Tracy Dunkelberger
	Executive Editor
	Advanced Programming and
	Distributed Architectures Team
	Macmillan Computer Publishing
	201 West 103rd Street
	Indianapolis, IN 46290 USA

INTRODUCTION

Suppose you have to learn C++ in a hurry. Perhaps you are already a C programmer, or you learned C++ some time back but need a quick review. Or perhaps just don't have time to wade through a full-scale primer. Or perhaps you just want to look up how to accomplish one particular technique.

Sams Teach Yourself C++ in 10 Minutes is designed to provide you with the essentials of this powerful language in short, quick, easy-to-digest lessons. You can't learn an entire programming language in 10 minutes, but you can learn a specific technique that quickly.

WELCOME TO C++ IN 10 MINUTES

Many professionals don't have the time to sit down for hours to learn what they need to know about programming. This 10-minute guide does not attempt to teach you everything about C++ in huge chapters you don't have time to read. Instead, it focuses on the most often-used aspects of the language, covering them in self-contained lessons designed to take 10 minutes or less to complete.

WHO SHOULD READ *SAMS TEACH YOURSELF C++ IN 10 MINUTES*?

This book is for anyone who

- Needs to learn the fundamentals of C++ quickly

- Wants to brush up on C++ skills

- Needs to look up a specific technique

- Wants to find out if C++ is "right for me"

WHAT IS COVERED IN THIS BOOK?

Sams Teach Yourself C++ In 10 Minutes covers all the essential features of this powerful language, including:

- Editing, compiling, and linking
- The structure of C++ programs
- Variables and constants
- Functions and parameters
- Classes and objects
- Pointers and references
- Conditional branching and looping
- Data structures and arrays
- Inheritance
- Encapsulation and data hiding
- Exceptions
- Templates
- Polymorphism and virtual functions

CONVENTIONS USED IN THIS BOOK

Each lesson in this book explains a different aspect of C++ programming. The following icons will help you identify how particular pieces of information are used in this book:

Tip Look here for ideas that cut corners and confusion.

Plain English New or unfamiliar terms are defined in (you got it) "plain English."

Caution This icon identifies areas where new users often run into trouble and offers practical solutions to those problems.

➡ A code continuation arrow indicates a line that continues. When you enter the code, type the two lines as one; do not divide them.

Lesson 1
What Is C++?

In this lesson, you will learn how to prepare, design, and start programming in C++.

Why C++ Is the Right Choice

C++ is the development language of choice for the majority of professional programmers because it offers fast, small programs developed in a robust and portable environment. Today's C++ tools make creating complex and powerful commercial applications a pretty straightforward exercise. In this first lesson, you will learn what you need to know to get started with programming in C++.

Preparing to Program

The first question to ask when preparing to design any program is, "What is the problem I'm trying to solve?" Every program should have a clear, well-articulated goal, and you'll find that even the simplest programs in this book will have one.

C++, ANSI C++, Windows, and Other Areas of Confusion

Sams Teach Yourself C++ In 10 Minutes makes no assumptions about your operating system. This book teaches ISO/ANSI standard C++ (which from now on I'll just call Standard C++).

Therefore, you won't see anything in this book about windows, list boxes, graphics and so forth. All that is operating system dependent (for example, Windows is different from the Mac). You'll see output accomplished through "standard output," (that is, just written as text to the screen).

YOUR COMPILER AND EDITOR

You can use this book with any editor and compiler, but I'll demonstrate everything using Microsoft's Visual C++ 6.0. I use the *Enterprise Edition*, which at the time of this writing costs about $1,200. Microsoft offers a series of less powerful versions of this compiler, including the Introductory Edition, which is available with *Sams Teach Yourself C++ In 21 Days, Complete Compiler Edition*. That book, which I also wrote, is targeted at readers who want more detail, and exercises at the end of each chapter, and who have more time to spend learning the language.

GETTING STARTED WITH A NEW PROJECT

Okay, time to get started. You're on your own installing the compiler, but it should be fairly straightforward. This section will describe how to get started with Visual C++. This is the development environment I use, but the general principals should apply whatever you are using.

To get started, choose **File/New** and you'll see the dialog box for creating new files, workspaces, and so forth, as shown in Figure 1.1.

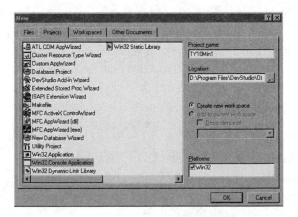

FIGURE 1.1   Starting a project in Visual C++.

There are lots of interesting things to see here, but we care about only a very small subset: we'll be creating nothing but Win32 Console Applications. Click the **Projects** tab and then click **Win32 Console Application**. Fill in a name for your project—for our purposes a project is just a "program." You can then click OK.

You'll be asked what kind of project you want; just choose the default, An Empty Project. If you have a different version of the Microsoft compiler, the screens may differ somewhat, but the choices should be pretty clear.

You are now in the Microsoft Editor. Read through the documentation. From here you can create .cpp files (source code files) and .h files (header files). You can compile, link, and run your programs. (I'll explain these steps in a moment.) Remember, when running your programs, press Control-F5, which will open an output window, display your results, and wait for you to hit a key before closing the window.

THE DEVELOPMENT CYCLE

If every program worked the first time you tried it, the complete development cycle would be: write the program, compile the source code, link the program, and run it. Unfortunately, almost every program, no matter how trivial, can and will have errors, or bugs, in it. Some bugs will cause the compile to fail, some will cause the link to fail, and some will only show up when you run the program.

Whatever the type of bug you find, you must fix it; and that involves editing your source code, recompiling and relinking, and then rerunning the program. This cycle is represented in Figure 1.2, which diagrams the steps in the development cycle.

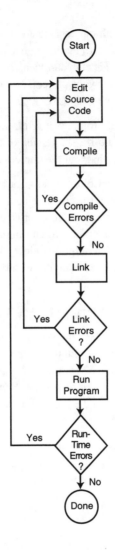

FIGURE 1.2   The steps in the development of a C++ program.

HELLO.CPP—YOUR FIRST C++ PROGRAM

Traditional programming books begin by writing the words Hello World to the screen, or a variation on that statement. This time-honored tradition is carried on here.

Open **File/New** and choose **C++ Source File**. Enter a name (I use *hello*). Enter the code shown in Listing 1.1 into the editor, exactly as shown, except do not enter the line numbers. When you are certain it is correct, save the file.

 Line Numbers in Code   The following listing contains line numbers on the left. These numbers are for reference within the book. They should not be typed in your editor. For example, in line 1 of Listing 1.1, you should enter:

```
#include <iostream.h>
```

LISTING 1.1   **HELLO.CPP, THE Hello World PROGRAM**

```
1: #include <iostream.h>
2:
3: int main()
4: {
5:     cout << "Hello World!\n";
6:     return 0;
7: }
```

Make certain you enter this exactly as shown. Pay careful attention to the punctuation. The << in line 5 is the redirection symbol, produced on most keyboards by holding the shift key and pressing the comma key twice. Line 5 ends with a semicolon; don't leave this off!

In C++, every character, including punctuation, is critical and must be entered exactly right. In addition, C++ is case sensitive, so return and Return are not the same.

COMPILE ERRORS

Compile-time errors can occur for any number of reasons. Usually they are a result of a typo or other inadvertent minor error. Good compilers will not only tell you what you did wrong, they'll point you to the exact place in your code where you made the mistake. The great ones will even suggest a remedy!

Punctuation Errors   While modern compilers do try to find the line on which your bug appears, the absence of a semicolon or closing brace can confuse the compiler and you may find it pointing to a line which is otherwise fine. Beware of punctuation errors, they can be tricky to find.

You can test this by intentionally putting an error into your program. If HELLO.CPP ran smoothly, edit it now and remove the closing brace on line 7. Your program will now look like Listing 1.2.

LISTING 1.2   DEMONSTRATION OF COMPILER ERROR

```
1: #include <iostream.h>
2:
3: int main()()
4: {
5:    cout << "Hello World!\n";
6:    return 0;
```

Recompile your program, and you should see an error that looks similar to

```
F:\Mcp\Tycpp10m\Source\List0102.cpp(8) :
➥fatal error C1004: unexpected end of file found
```

This error tells you the file and line number of the problem and what the problem is. Earlier versions of Visual C++ responded to the same source code with this error:

```
Hello.cpp, line 5: Compound statement missing
➥terminating } in function main().
```

This older error was considerably more cryptic and pointed you to \ line 5. The compiler wasn't sure if you intended to put the closing brace before or after the cout statement on line 5. Sometimes the errors just get you to the general vicinity of the problem. If a compiler could perfectly identify every problem, it would fix the code itself.

In this lesson, you learned how to prepare to program in C++.

Lesson 2

What is a C++ Program?

In this lesson, you will learn the parts of a C++ program, how the parts work together, and what a function is and what it does.

The Parts of a Simple Program

Before we dive into the details of C++, classes, variables, and so forth, let's take ten minutes to get a sense of how a program fits together.

The simple program from the first lesson, HELLO.CPP, had many interesting parts. This section will review this program in more detail. Listing 2.1 reproduces the original version of HELLO.CPP for your convenience.

LISTING 2.1   HELLO.CPP DEMONSTRATES THE PARTS OF A C++ PROGRAM

```
1: #include <iostream.h>
2:
3: int main()
4: {
5:     cout << "Hello World!\n";
6:     return 0;
7: }

Hello World!
```

On line 1, the file iostream.h is included in the file. As far as the compiler is concerned, it's as if you typed the entire contents of the file iostream.h right into the top of HELLO.CPP.

EXAMINING THE #include, CHARACTER BY CHARACTER

The first character is the # symbol, which is a signal to the *preprocessor*. The job of the preprocessor is to read through your source code looking for lines that begin with the pound symbol (#), and when it finds one, to modify the code.

include is a preprocessor instruction that says, "What follows is a file-name. Find that file and read it in right here." The angle brackets around the filename tell the preprocessor, "Look in all the usual places for this file." If your compiler is set up correctly, the angle brackets will cause the preprocessor to look for the file Iostream.H in the directory that holds all the H files for your compiler. The file Iostream.H (Input-Output-STREAM) is used by cout, which assists with writing to the screen.

The effect of line 1 is to include the file Iostream.H into this program as if you had typed it in yourself.

LINE BY LINE ANALYSIS

Line 3 begins the actual program with a function named main(). Every C++ program has a main() function. In general, a function is a block of code that performs one or more actions. Functions are invoked, (some programmers say they are called) by other functions, but main() is spe-cial. When your program starts, main() is called automatically.

main(), like all functions, must state what kind of value it will return. Once again, main() is special, it will always return int. Returning a value from a function will be discussed in detail in Lesson 4, "Statements."

All functions begin with an opening brace ({) and end with a closing brace (}). The braces for the main() function are on lines 4 and 7. Everything between the opening and closing braces is considered a part of the function.

cout is used to print a message to the screen.

The final two characters, \n, tell cout to put a new line after the words Hello World! On line 6 we call return 0. This returns control to the operating system (Windows).

The Meaningless Zero   The zero is a meaningless value no longer used very often (on Unix and DOS it was at times used in batch files to signal success or failure of a program).

The main() function ends on line 7 with the closing brace.

COMMENTS

A *comment* is text you add to explain (to yourself or other programmers) what is happening in your code. The comment has no effect; it serves only as documentation.

There are two types of comments in C++. The double-slash (//) comment, which will be referred to as a C++-style comment, tells the compiler to ignore everything that follows the slashes until the end of the line.

The C-style slash-star (/*) comment mark tells the compiler to ignore everything that follows until it finds a star-slash (*/) comment mark.

FUNCTIONS

While main() is a function, it is an unusual one, because it is called automatically when you start your program. All other functions are called by your own code, as your program runs.

A program is executed line by line in the order it appears in your source code, until a function is called. Then the program branches off to execute the function. When the function finishes, it returns control to the next line in the calling function.

When a program needs a service performed, it calls a function to perform the service and, when the function returns, the program resumes where it was just before the function was called.

Functions either return a value or they return void, meaning they return nothing. Note that main() always returns an int.

A function that adds two integers might return the sum and, thus, would be defined to return an integer value. A function that just prints a message has nothing to return and would be declared to return void.

Functions consist of a header and a body. The header consists, in turn, of the return type, the function name, and the parameters to that function. The parameters to a function allow values to be passed into the function. Thus, if the function were to add two numbers, the numbers would be the parameters to the function. Here's a typical function header:

```
int Sum(int a, int b)
```

A *parameter* is a declaration of what type of value will be passed in; the actual value passed in by the calling function is called the *argument*. Many programmers use these two terms, parameters and arguments, as synonyms.

The name of the function and its parameters (that is the header without the return value) is called the *function's signature*.

The body of a function consists of an opening brace, zero or more statements, and a closing brace. The statements constitute the work of the function. A function may return a value using a `return` statement. This statement will also cause the function to exit. If you don't put a `return` statement into your function, it will automatically return void at the end of the function. The value returned must be of the type declared in the function header.

Listing 2.2 demonstrates a function that takes two integer parameters and returns an integer value. Don't worry about the syntax or the specifics of how to work with integer values for now That will be covered soon.

LISTING 2.2   FUNC.CPP DEMONSTRATES A SIMPLE FUNCTION

```
1:     #include <iostream.h>
2:     int Add (int x, int y)
3:     {
4:
5:         cout << "In Add(), received " << x << "
       ➥ and " << y << "\n";
6:         return (x+y);
7:     }
8:
9:     int main()
10:    {
11:        cout << "I'm in main()!\n";
12:        int a, b, c;
```

```
13:        cout << "Enter two numbers: ";
14:        cin >> a;
15:        cin >> b;
16:        cout << "\nCalling Add()\n";
17:        c=Add(a,b);
18:        cout << "\nBack in main().\n";
19:        cout << "c was set to " << c;
20:        cout << "\nExiting...\n\n";
21:        return 0;
22:    }
```

OUTPUT

```
I'm in main()!
Enter two numbers: 3 5

Calling Add()
In Add(), received 3 and 5

Back in main().
c was set to 8
Exiting...
```

The function Add() is defined on line 2. It takes two integer parameters and returns an integer value. The program itself begins on line 11 where it prints a message. The program prompts the user for two numbers (lines 13 to 15). The user types each number, separated by a space, and then presses Enter. Main() passes the two numbers typed in by the user as arguments to the Add() function on line 17.

Processing branches to the Add() function, which starts on line 2. The parameters a and b are printed and then added together. The result is returned on line 6, and the function returns.

In lines 14 and 15, the cin object is used to obtain a number for the variables a and b, and cout is used to write the values to the screen. Variables and other aspects of this program will be explored in depth in the next few days.

In this lesson, you learned the parts of a C++ program and how those parts work together. You also learned what a function is and how to use it.

LESSON 3
VARIABLES

In this lesson, you will learn how to declare and define variables and constants, how to assign values to variables and manipulate those values, and how to write the value of a variable to the screen.

WHAT IS A VARIABLE?

Programs need a way to store the data they use. Variables and constants offer various ways to work with numbers and other values.

From a programmer's point of view, a *variable* is a location in your computer's memory in which you can store a value and from which you can later retrieve that value.

To understand this, you must first understand a bit about how computer memory works. Your computer's memory can be thought of as a series of cubbyholes, all lined up in a long row. Each cubbyhole—or memory location—is numbered sequentially. These numbers are known as memory addresses.

Variables not only have addresses, they have names. For example, you might create a variable named myAge. Your variable is a label on one of these cubbyholes so that you can find it easily, without knowing its actual memory address.

Figure 3.1 is a schematic representation of this idea. As you can see from the figure, we've declared a variable named myVariable. myVariable starts at memory address 103.

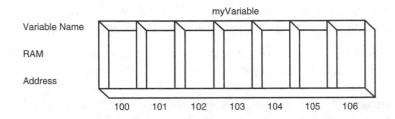

myVariable

Variable Name

RAM

Address

| 100 | 101 | 102 | 103 | 104 | 105 | 106 |

FIGURE 3.1   A schematic representation of memory.

RAM (Random Access Memory)   When you run your program, it is loaded into RAM from the disk file. All variables are created in RAM as well. When programmers talk of memory, it is usually RAM they are referring to.

SETTING ASIDE MEMORY

When you define a variable in C++, you must tell the compiler not only what its name is, but also what kind of information it will hold: integer, character, and so forth. We call this the variable's *type*. The type of the variable tells the compiler how much room to set aside in memory to hold the variable's value.

Each cubby is 1 byte large. If the type of variable you create is 2 bytes in size, it needs 2 bytes of memory, or two cubbies. The type of the variable (for example, int) tells the compiler how much memory (how many cubbyholes) to set aside for the variable.

Because computers use bits and bytes to represent values, and because memory is measured in bytes, it is important that you understand and are comfortable with these concepts.

SIZE OF INTEGERS

A char variable (used to hold characters) is most often 1 byte long. A short int is 2 bytes on most computers, a long int is usually 4 bytes, and an int (without the keyword short or long) can be 2 or 4 bytes. If you are running Windows 95, Windows 98, or Windows NT, you can count on your int being 4 bytes as long as you use a modern compiler.

Listing 3.1 should help you determine the exact size of these types on your computer using your particular compiler

LISTING 3.1   DETERMINES THE SIZE OF VARIABLE TYPES ON YOUR COMPUTER

```
1:    #include <iostream.h>
2:
3:    int main()
4:    {
5:        cout << "The size of an int is:\t\t"
        ➥<< sizeof(int)     << " bytes.\n";
6:        cout << "The size of a short int is:\t"
        ➥<< sizeof(short)  << " bytes.\n";
7:        cout << "The size of a long int is:\t"
        ➥<< sizeof(long)   << " bytes.\n";
8:        cout << "The size of a char is:\t\t"
        ➥<< sizeof(char)   << " bytes.\n";
9:        cout << "The size of a bool is:\t\t"
        ➥<< sizeof(bool)   << " bytes.\n";
10:        cout << "The size of a float is:\t\t"
        ➥<< sizeof(float)  << " bytes.\n";
11:        cout << "The size of a double is:\t"
        ➥<< sizeof(double) << " bytes.\n";
12:
13:        return 0;
14:    }
```

OUTPUT

```
The size of an int is         4 bytes.
The size of a short int is    2 bytes.
The size of a long int is     4 bytes.
The size of a char is         1 bytes.
The size of a bool is         1 bytes.

The size of a float is        4 bytes.
The size of a double is       8 bytes.
```

signed AND unsigned

In addition, most of these types come in two varieties: signed and unsigned. The idea here is that sometimes you need negative numbers, and sometimes you don't. Integers (short and long) without the word "unsigned" are assumed to be signed. signed integers are either negative or positive. unsigned integers are always positive.

> **Use int for Number Variables** For most programs, most of the time, you can simply declare your number variables to be `int`—that is signed integers.

FUNDAMENTAL VARIABLE TYPES

Several other variable types are built into C++. They can be conveniently divided into integer variables (the type discussed so far), floating-point variables, and character variables.

> **Floating-Point and Character Variables** Floating-point variables have values that can be expressed as fractions—that is, they are real numbers. Character variables hold a single byte and are used for holding the 256 characters and symbols of the ASCII and extended ASCII character sets.
>
> **The ASCII Character Set** The set of characters standardized for use on computers. ASCII is an acronym for American Standard Code for Information Interchange. Nearly every computer operating system supports ASCII, though many support other international character sets as well.

The types of variables used in C++ programs are described in Table 3.1. This table shows the variable type, how much room this book assumes it takes in memory, and what kinds of values can be stored in these variables. The values that can be stored are determined by the size of the variable types, so check your output from Listing 3.1.

TABLE 3.1 VARIABLE TYPES

TYPE	SIZE	VALUES
unsigned short int	2 bytes	0 to 65,535
short int	2 bytes	−32,768 to 32,767

continues

TABLE 3.1   CONTINUED

TYPE	SIZE	VALUES
unsigned long int	4 bytes	0 to 4,294,967,295
long int	4 bytes	–2,147,483,648 to 2,147,483,647
char	1 byte	256 character values
bool	1 byte	true or false
float	4 bytes	1.2e–38 to 3.4e38
double	8 bytes	2.2e–308 to 1.8e308

 Just Use int   If you are creating an int, don't worry about short vs. long; just use int. With a modern compiler, this will create a long int, which will be fine 99% of the time.

DEFINING A VARIABLE

You create, or define, a variable by stating its type, followed by one or more spaces, followed by the variable name and a semicolon. The variable name can be virtually any combination of letters, but cannot contain spaces. Legal variable names include x, J23qrsnf, and myAge. Good variable names tell you what the variables are used for; using good names makes it easier to understand the flow of your program.

CASE SENSITIVITY

C++ is *case-sensitive*. In other words, uppercase and lowercase letters are considered to be different. A variable named age is different from Age, which is different from AGE.

KEYWORDS

Some words are reserved by C++, and you may not use them as variable names. These are keywords used by the compiler to control your program.

Keywords include `if`, `while`, `for`, and `main`. Your compiler manual should provide a complete list, but generally, any reasonable name for a variable is almost certainly not a keyword.

CREATING MORE THAN ONE VARIABLE AT A TIME

You can create more than one variable of the same type in one statement by writing the type and then the variable names, separated by commas. For example

```
unsigned int myAge, myWeight;    // two unsigned int variables
long area, width, length;        // three longs
```

ASSIGNING VALUES TO YOUR VARIABLES

You assign a value to a variable by using the assignment operator (`=`). Thus, you would assign 5 to `Width` by writing

```
unsigned short Width;
Width = 5;
```

You can combine these steps and initialize `Width` when you define it by writing

```
unsigned short Width = 5;
```

CONSTANTS

Like variables, *constants* are data storage locations. But variables vary; constants, on the other hand, as you may have guessed, do not vary.

You must initialize a constant when you create it, and you cannot assign a new value later; once a constant is initialized its value is, in a word, constant.

LITERAL CONSTANTS

C++ has two types of constants: *literal* and *symbolic*.

A *literal constant* is a value typed directly into your program wherever it is needed. For example

```
int myAge = 39;
```

myAge is a variable, of type int; 39 is a literal constant. You can't assign a value to 39, and its value can't be changed.

SYMBOLIC CONSTANTS

A *symbolic constant* is a constant that is represented by a name, just as a variable is. Unlike a variable, however, after a constant is initialized, its value can't be changed.

If your program has one integer variable named students and another named classes, you can compute how many students you have, given a known number of classes; if you knew there were 15 students per class:

```
students = classes * 15;
```

 How to Multiply   Multiplication is indicated by *.

In this example, 15 is a literal constant. Your code would be easier to read, and easier to maintain, if you substituted a symbolic constant for this value:

```
students = classes * studentsPerClass
```

If you later decided to change the number of students in each class, you could do so where you define the constant studentsPerClass without having to make a change every place you used that value.

DEFINING CONSTANTS WITH #define

To define a constant the old-fashioned, evil, politically-incorrect way, you would enter:

```
#define studentsPerClass 15
```

Note that `studentsPerClass` is of no particular type (`int`, `char`, and so on). `#define` does a simple text substitution. Every time the preprocessor sees the word `studentsPerClass`, it puts 15 in the text.

Because the preprocessor runs before the compiler, your compiler never sees your constant; it sees the number 15.

DEFINING CONSTANTS WITH `const`

Although `#define` works, there is a new, better, less fattening, and more tasteful way to define constants in C++:

```
const unsigned short int studentsPerClass = 15;
```

This example also declares a symbolic constant named `studentsPerClass`, but this time `studentsPerClass` is typed as an `unsigned short int`.

This is longer to type, but offers several advantages. The biggest difference is that this constant has a type, and the compiler can enforce that it is used according to its type.

ENUMERATED CONSTANTS

Enumerated constants create a set of constants with a range of values. For example, you can declare COLOR to be an enumeration, and you can define that there are five values for COLOR: RED, BLUE, GREEN, WHITE, and BLACK.

The syntax for enumerated constants is to write the keyword enum, followed by the type name, an open brace, each of the legal values separated by a comma, and finally a closing brace and a semicolon. Here's an example:

```
enum COLOR { RED, BLUE, GREEN, WHITE, BLACK };
```

This statement performs two tasks:

1. It makes COLOR the name of an enumeration, that is, a new type.

2. It makes RED a symbolic constant with the value 0, BLUE a symbolic constant with the value 1, GREEN a symbolic constant with the value 2, and so forth.

Every enumerated constant has an integer value. If you don't specify otherwise, the first constant will have the value 0, and the rest will count up from there. Any one of the constants can be initialized with a particular value, however, and those that are not initialized will count upward from the ones before them. Thus, if you write

```
enum Color { RED=100, BLUE, GREEN=500, WHITE, BLACK=700 };
```

then RED will have the value 100; BLUE, the value 101; GREEN, the value 500; WHITE, the value 501; and BLACK, the value 700.

In this lesson, you learned how to declare and define variables and constants and how to assign values to these variables and constants.

LESSON 4
STATEMENTS

In this lesson, you will learn what statements and expressions are and how to work with operators.

STATEMENTS

A program is really nothing more than a set of commands executed in sequence. A *statement* controls the sequence of execution, evaluates an expression, or does nothing (the `null` statement). All C++ statements end with a semicolon.

A common simple statement is an assignment:

```
x = a + b;
```

Unlike algebra, this statement does not mean that x equals a+b. This is read, "Assign the value of the sum of a and b to x," or "Assign to x, a+b." Even though this statement is doing two things, it is one statement and, therefore, has one semicolon. The assignment operator assigns whatever is on the right side to whatever is on the left side.

WHITESPACE

Spaces, along with tabs and new lines are called *whitespace*. Extra white-space is generally ignored by the compiler; any place you see a single space you can just as easily put a tab or a new line. Whitespace is added only to make a program more readable by humans; the compiler won't notice.

The assignment statement could have been written as

```
x=a+b;
```

or as

```
x                          =a
+           b              ;
```

Use Whitespace to Make Your Code More Legible
Although this last variation is perfectly legal, it is also perfectly foolish. Whitespace can be used to make your programs more readable and easier to maintain, or it can be used to create indecipherable code. In this, as in all things, C++ provides the power; you supply the judgment.

COMPOUND STATEMENTS

Any place you can put a single statement, you can put a compound statement.

Compound Statement   A statement that begins with an opening brace ({) and ends with a closing brace (}).

Although every statement in a compound statement must end with a semicolon, the compound statement itself does not end with a semicolon. For example:

```
{
    temp = a;
    a = b;
    b = temp;
}
```

This compound statement swaps the values in the variables a and b.

EXPRESSIONS

Anything that returns a value is an *expression* in C++.

OPERATORS

An *operator* is a symbol that causes the compiler to take an action.

ASSIGNMENT OPERATOR

The *assignment operator* (=) causes the operand on the left side of the assignment operator to have its value changed to the value on the right side of the assignment operator. The expression

```
x = a + b;
```

assigns the value that is the result of adding a and b to the operand x.

An operand that can legally be on the left side of an assignment operator is called an l-value. That which can be on the right side is called (you guessed it) an r-value.

Constants are r-values; they cannot be l-values. Thus, you can write

```
x = 35;          // ok
```

but you can't legally write

```
35 = x;          // error, not an lvalue!
```

l-values and r-values   An l-value is an operand that can be on the left side of an expression. An r-value is an operand that can be on the right side of an expression. Note that all l-values are r-values, but not all r-values are l-values. An example of an r-value that is not an l-value is a literal. Thus, you can write x = 5;, but you cannot write 5 = x;.

MATHEMATICAL OPERATORS

There are five mathematical operators: addition (+), subtraction (-), multiplication (*), division (/), and modulus (%). Addition, subtraction, and multiplication act pretty much as you might expect. Not so with division.

Integer division is somewhat different from everyday division. When you divide 21 by 4, the result is a real number (a number with a fraction). Integers don't have fractions, and so the "remainder" is lopped off. The value returned by 21 / 4 is 5.

The modulus operator (%) returns the remainder value of integer division. Thus 21 % 4 is 1, because 21 / 4 is 5 with a remainder of 1.

Surprisingly, finding the modulus can be very useful. For example, you might want to print a statement on every 10th action.

It turns out that any number % 10 will return 0 if the number is a multiple of 10. Thus 20%10 is zero. 30%10 is zero.

COMBINING THE ASSIGNMENT AND MATHEMATICAL OPERATORS

It is not uncommon to want to add a value to a variable and then to assign the result back into the variable. In C++ you can write

```
myAge += 2;
```

This increases the value in myAge by 2.

INCREMENT AND DECREMENT

The most common value to add (or subtract) and then reassign into a variable is 1. In C++ increasing a value by 1 is called *incrementing*, and decreasing by 1 is called *decrementing*. There are special operators to perform these actions.

The increment operator (++) increases the value of the variable by 1, and the decrement operator (--) decreases it by 1. Thus, if you have a variable, C, and you want to increment it, you would use this statement:

```
C++;            // Start with C and increment it.
```

PREFIX AND POSTFIX

Both the increment operator (++) and the decrement operator (- -) come in two flavors: *prefix* and *postfix*.

Prefix The operator is written before the variable name (++myAge).

Postfix The operator is written after the variable name (myAge++).

In a simple statement, it doesn't much matter which you use, but in a complex statement, when you are incrementing (or decrementing) a variable and then assigning the result to another variable, it matters very much. The prefix operator is evaluated before the assignment, the postfix is evaluated after.

The semantics of prefix is this: increment the value and then fetch it. The semantics of postfix is different: fetch the value and then increment the original.

This can be confusing at first, but if x is an integer whose value is 5 and you write

```
int a = ++x;
```

you have told the compiler to increment x (making it 6) and then fetch that value and assign it to a. Thus a is now 6 and x is now 6.

If, after doing this, you write

```
int b = x++;
```

you have now told the compiler to fetch the value in x (6) and assign it to b, and then go back and increment x. Thus, b is now 6 but x is now 7. Listing 4.1 shows the use and implications of both types.

LISTING 4.1   DEMONSTRATES PREFIX AND POSTFIX OPERATORS

```
1:  // Listing 4.1 - demonstrates use of
2:  // prefix and postfix increment and
3:  // decrement operators
4:  #include <iostream.h>
5:  int main()
6:  {
7:      int myAge = 39;        // initialize two integers
8:      int yourAge = 39;
9:      cout << "I am:\t" << myAge << "\tyears old.\n";
10:     cout << "You are:\t" << yourAge << "\tyears old\n";
11:     myAge++;               // postfix increment
12:     ++yourAge;             // prefix increment
13:     cout << "One year passes...\n";
14:     cout << "I am:\t" << myAge << "\tyears old.\n";
15:     cout << "You are:\t" << yourAge << "\tyears old\n";
16:     cout << "Another year passes\n";
17:     cout << "I am:\t" << myAge++ << "\tyears old.\n";
18:     cout << "You are:\t" << ++yourAge << "\tyears old\n";
19:     cout << "Let's print it again.\n";
20:     cout << "I am:\t" << myAge << "\tyears old.\n";
21:     cout << "You are:\t" << yourAge << "\tyears old\n";
22:     return 0;
23: }
```

OUTPUT

```
I am        39 years old
You are     39 years old
One year passes
I am        40 years old
You are     40 years old
Another year passes
I am        40 years old
You are     41 years old
Let's print it again
I am        41 years old
You are     41 years old
```

On lines 7 and 8, two integer variables are declared, and each is initialized with the value 39. Their value is printed on lines 9 and 10.

On line 11, myAge is incremented using the postfix increment operator, and on line 12, yourAge is incremented using the prefix increment operator. The results are printed on lines 14 and 15, and they are identical (both 40).

On line 17, myAge is incremented as part of the printing statement, using the postfix increment operator. Because it is postfix, the increment happens after the print, and so the value 40 is printed again. In contrast, on line 18 yourAge is incremented using the prefix increment operator. Thus, it is incremented before being printed, and the value displays as 41.

Finally, on lines 20 and 21, the values are printed again. Because the increment statement has completed, the value in myAge is now 41 as is the value in yourAge.

PRECEDENCE

In the complex statement

```
x = 5 + 3 * 8;
```

which is performed first, the addition or the multiplication? If the addition is performed first, the answer is 8 * 8, or 64. If the multiplication is performed first, the answer is 5 + 24, or 29.

 Precedence Every operator has a precedence value, and the complete list is shown in Appendix A, "Operator Precedence." Multiplication has a higher precedence than addition, and thus the value of the expression is 29.

When two mathematical operators have the same precedence, they are performed in left-to-right order. Thus,

```
x = 5 + 3 + 8 * 9 + 6 * 4;
```

is evaluated multiplication first, left to right. Thus, 8*9 = 72, and 6*4 = 24. Now the expression is essentially

```
x = 5 + 3 + 72 + 24;
```

Now the addition, left to right, is 5 + 3 = 8; 8 + 72 = 80; 80 + 24 = 104.

Be careful with this. Some operators, such as assignment, are evaluated in right-to-left order! In any case, what if the precedence order doesn't meet your needs? Consider the expression

```
TotalSeconds = NumMinutesToThink +
➥NumMinutesToType * 60
```

In this expression you do not want to multiply the `NumMinutesToType` variable by `60` and then add it to `NumMinutesToThink`. You want to add the two variables to get the total number of minutes, and then you want to multiply that number by `60` to get the total seconds.

In this case, you use parentheses to change the precedence order. Items in parentheses are evaluated at a higher precedence than any of the mathematical operators. Thus,

```
TotalSeconds = (NumMinutesToThink +
➥NumMinutesToType) * 60
```

will accomplish what you want.

NESTING PARENTHESES

For complex expressions you might need to nest parentheses one within another. For example, you might need to compute the total seconds and then compute the total number of people who are involved before multiplying seconds times people:

```
TotalPersonSeconds = ( ( (NumMinutesToThink +
➥NumMinutesToType) * 60)
➥ * (PeopleInTheOffice + PeopleOnVacation) )
```

This complicated expression is read from the inside out. First, `NumMinutesToThink` is added to `NumMinutesToType`, because these are in the innermost parentheses. Then this sum is multiplied by `60`. Next, `PeopleInTheOffice` is added to `PeopleOnVacation`. Finally, the total number of people found is multiplied by the total number of seconds.

This example raises an important issue. This expression is easy for a computer to understand, but very difficult for a human to read, understand, or modify. Here is the same expression rewritten, using some temporary integer variables:

```
TotalMinutes = NumMinutesToThink + NumMinutesToType;
TotalSeconds = TotalMinutes * 60;
TotalPeople = PeopleInTheOffice + PeopleOnVacation;
TotalPersonSeconds = TotalPeople * TotalSeconds;
```

This example takes longer to write and uses more temporary variables than the preceding example, but it is far easier to understand. Add a comment at the top to explain what this code does, and change the 60 to a symbolic constant. You then will have code that is easy to understand and maintain.

THE NATURE OF TRUTH

In previous versions of C++, all truth and falsity was represented by integers, but the new ISO/ANSI standard has introduced a new type: bool. This new type has two possible values, false or true.

Every expression can be evaluated for its truth or falsity. Expressions which evaluate mathematically to zero will return false, all others will return true.

RELATIONAL OPERATORS

The relational operators are used to determine whether two numbers are equal or if one is greater or less than the other. Every relational expression returns either true or false. The relational operators are presented in Table 4.1.

There are six relational operators: equals (==), less than (<), greater than (>), (greater than operator)> less than or equal to (<=), greater than or equal to (>=), and not equals (!=). Table 4.1 shows each relational operator, its use, and a sample code use.

TABLE 4.1   THE RELATIONAL OPERATORS

NAME	OPERATOR	SAMPLE	EVALUATES
Equals	==	100 == 50;	false
		50 == 50;	true
Not Equals	!=	100 != 50;	true
		50 != 50;	false
Greater Than	>	100 > 50;	true
		50 > 50;	false
Greater Than or Equals	>=	100 >= 50;	true
		50 >= 50;	true
Less Than	<	100 < 50;	false
		50 < 50;	false
Less Than or Equals	<=	100 <= 50;	false
		50 <= 50;	true

In this lesson, you learned what statements are, what expressions are, and how to work with operators.

LESSON 5
THE if STATEMENT

In this lesson, you will learn how to use the if statement and how to use relational operators to compare two values.

THE if STATEMENT

Normally, your program flows along line by line in the order in which it appears in your source code. There are times, however, when you want to take one action if a particular condition has been met; otherwise, you'd like to take a different action.

The if statement enables you to test for a condition (such as whether two variables are equal) and branch to different parts of your code depending on the result.

The simplest form of an if statement is this:

```
if (expression)
    statement;
```

The expression in the parentheses can be any expression at all, but it usually contains one of the relational expressions. If the expression is false the statement is skipped. Look at this example:

```
if (bigNumber > smallNumber)
    bigNumber = smallNumber;
```

This code compares bigNumber and smallNumber. If bigNumber is larger, the second line sets its value to the value of smallNumber.

THE else CLAUSE

Often your program will want to take one branch if your condition is true, another if it is false.

The method shown so far, testing first one condition and then the other, works fine but is a bit cumbersome. The keyword `else` can make for far more readable code:

```
if (expression)
     statement;
else
     statement;
```

ADVANCED `if` STATEMENTS

It is worth noting that any statement can be used in an `if` or `else` clause, even another `if` or `else` statement. Thus, you might see complex `if` statements in the following form:

```
if (expression1)
{
    if (expression2)
         statement1;
    else
    {
        if (expression3)
             statement2;
        else
             statement3;
    }
}
else
    statement4;
```

This cumbersome `if` statement says, "If expression1 is true and expression2 is true, execute statement1. If expression1 is true but expression2 is not true, then if expression3 is true, execute statement2. If expression1 is true but expression2 and expression3 are false, execute statement3. Finally, if expression1 is not true, execute statement4." As you can see, complex `if` statements can be confusing!

USE BRACES IN NESTED `if` STATEMENTS

Although it is legal to leave out the braces on an `if` statement that is only a single statement, and it is legal to nest `if` statements, such as

```
if (x > y)              // if x is bigger than y
   if (x < z)           // and if x is smaller than z
      x = y;            // then set x to the value in y
```

when writing large nested statements, doing so can cause enormous confusion.

 Use if Statements Carefully   Whitespace and indentation are conveniences for the programmer; they make no difference to the compiler. It is easy to confuse the logic and inadvertently assign an else statement to the wrong if statement.

Listing 5.1 gives an example of such a complex if statement.

LISTING 5.1   A COMPLEX, NESTED if STATEMENT

```
1:  // Listing 5.1 - a complex nested
2:  // if statement
3:  #include <iostream.h>
4:  int main()
5:  {
6:      // Ask for two numbers
7:      // Assign the numbers to bigNumber and littleNumber
8:      // If bigNumber is bigger than littleNumber,
9:      // see if they are evenly divisible
10:     // If they are, see if they are the same number
11:
12:     int firstNumber, secondNumber;
13:     cout << "Enter two numbers.\nFirst: ";
14:     cin >> firstNumber;
15:     cout << "\nSecond: ";
16:     cin >> secondNumber;
17:     cout << "\n\n";
18:
19:     if (firstNumber >= secondNumber)
20:     {
21:       if ( (firstNumber % secondNumber) == 0)
22:       {
23:             if (firstNumber == secondNumber)
24:                 cout << "They are the same!\n";
```

continues

LISTING 5.1   CONTINUED

```
25:                 else
26:                     cout << "They are evenly divisible!\n";
27:         }
28:     else
29:         cout << "They are not evenly divisible!\n";
30:   }
31:   else
32:     cout << "Hey! The second one is larger!\n";
33:   return 0;
34: }
```

OUTPUT

```
Enter two numbers.
First: 10
Second: 2
They are evenly divisible!
```

Two numbers are prompted for and then compared. The first if statement, on line 19, checks to ensure that the first number is greater than or equal to the second. If not, the else clause on line 31 is executed.

If the first if is true, the block of code beginning on line 20 is executed, and the second if statement is tested on line 21. This checks to see whether the first number modulo the second number yields no remainder. If so, the numbers are either evenly divisible or equal. The if statement on line 23 checks for equality and displays the appropriate message either way.

If the if statement on line 21 fails, the else statement on line 28 is executed.

LOGICAL OPERATORS

Often you want to ask more than one relational question at a time. "Is it true that x is greater than y, and also true that y is greater than z?" A program might need to determine that both of these conditions are true, or that some other condition is true, in order to take an action.

Imagine a sophisticated alarm system that has this logic: "If the door alarm sounds AND it is after six p.m. AND it is NOT a holiday, OR if it is a weekend, then call the police." The three logical operators of C++ are used to make this kind of evaluation. These operators are listed in Table 5.1.

TABLE 5.1   THE LOGICAL OPERATORS

OPERATOR	SYMBOL	EXAMPLE
AND expression2	&&	expression1 &&
OR expression2	¦¦	expression1 ¦¦
NOT	!	!expression

LOGICAL AND

A logical AND statement evaluates two expressions, and if both expressions are true, the logical AND statement is true as well. If it is true that you are hungry, AND it is true that you have money, THEN it is true that you can buy lunch. Thus

```
if ( (x == 5) && (y == 5) )
```

would evaluate true if both x and y are equal to 5, and it would evaluate false if either one is not equal to 5. Note that both sides must be true for the entire expression to be true.

Note that the logical AND is two & symbols.

LOGICAL OR

A logical OR statement evaluates two expressions. If either one is true, the expression is true. If you have money OR you have a credit card, you can pay the bill. You don't need both money and a credit card; you need only one, although having both would be fine as well. Thus

```
if ( (x == 5) ¦¦ (y == 5) )
```

evaluates true if either x or y is equal to 5, or if both are equal to five. In fact, if x is equal to five, the compiler will never check on y at all!

Note that the logical OR is two ¦¦ symbols.

LOGICAL NOT

A logical NOT statement evaluates true if the expression being tested is false. Again, if the expression being tested is false, the value of the test is true! Thus

```
if ( !(x == 5) )
```

is true only if x is not equal to 5. This is exactly the same as writing

```
if (x != 5)
```

In this lesson you learned how to use the if statement, and how to use relational operators to compare two values.

LESSON 6
FUNCTIONS

In this lesson, you will learn what a function is and what its parts are, how to declare and define functions, how to pass parameters into functions, and how to return a value from a function.

WHAT IS A FUNCTION?

When people talk about C++ they mention objects first. Yet objects rely on functions to get their work done. A *function* is, in effect, a subprogram that can act on data and return a value. Every C++ program has at least one function, main(). When your program starts, main() is called automatically. main() might call other functions, some of which might call still others.

Each function has its own name, and when that name is encountered, the execution of the program branches to the body of that function. When the function returns, execution resumes on the next line of the calling function. This flow is illustrated in Figure 6.1.

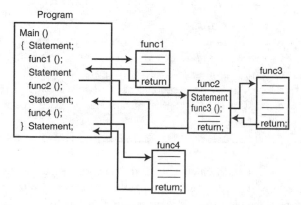

FIGURE 6.1 When a program calls a function, execution switches to the function and then resumes at the line after the function call.

A well-designed function will perform a specific task. That means it does one thing, does it well, and then returns.

Complicated tasks should be broken down into multiple functions, and then each can be called in turn. This makes your code easier to understand and easier to maintain.

DECLARING AND DEFINING FUNCTIONS

Before you can use a function, you must first *declare* the function and then *define* the function.

A function declaration, or prototype, is a statement and ends with a semicolon. It consists of the function's return type, name, and parameter list. Figure 6.2 illustrates the parts of the function prototype.

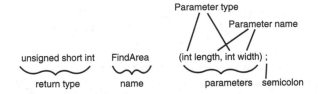

FIGURE 6.2   Parts of a function prototype.

Parameters or Arguments?   The values passed to a function are its arguments. Arguments come in two flavors: formal and actual. Formal arguments are also called parameters. Actual arguments are the values passed in during a call to the procedure. Most programmers use the terms parameter and argument interchangeably.

The definition of a function consists of the function header and its body. The header is exactly like the function prototype, except that the parameters must be named and there is no terminating semicolon.

The body of the function is a set of statements enclosed in braces. Figure 6.3 shows the header and body of a function.

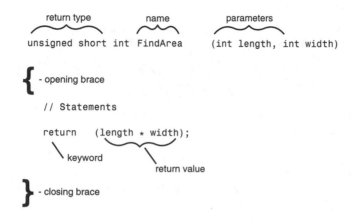

return type   name   parameters

unsigned short int FindArea   (int length, int width)

{ - opening brace

    // Statements

    return (length * width);
         \ keyword   \ return value

} - closing brace

FIGURE 6.3   The header and body of a function.

LOCAL VARIABLES

Not only can you pass in variables to the function, but you also can declare variables within the body of the function. This is done using *local variables*.

 Local Variables   Variables that exist only locally within the function itself. When the function returns, the local variables are no longer available.

Variables defined outside of any function have *global* scope and thus are available from any function in the program, including main(). In C++, global variables are avoided because they can create very confusing code that is hard to maintain.

FUNCTION STATEMENTS

There is virtually no limit to the number or types of statements that can be in a function body.

On the other hand, well-designed functions tend to be small. The vast majority of functions will be just a handful of lines of code.

FUNCTION ARGUMENTS

Function arguments do not have to all be the same type. It is perfectly reasonable to write a function that takes an integer, two longs, and a character as its arguments.

Any valid C++ expression can be a function argument, including constants, mathematical and logical expressions, and other functions that return a value.

USING FUNCTIONS AS PARAMETERS TO FUNCTIONS

Although it is legal to use a function that returns a value as a parameter to another function, it can make for code that is hard to read and hard to debug.

As an example, say you have the functions `double()`, `triple()`, `square()`, and `cube()`, each of which returns a value. You could write

```
Answer = (double(triple(square(cube(myValue)))));
```

This statement takes a variable, `myValue`, and passes it as an argument to the function `cube()`, whose return value is passed as an argument to the function `square()`, whose return value is in turn passed to `triple()`, and that return value is passed to `double()`. The return value of this doubled, tripled, squared, and cubed number is now passed to `Answer`.

It is difficult to be certain what this code does (was the value tripled before or after it was squared?), and if the answer is wrong it will be hard to figure out which function failed.

An alternative is to assign each step to its own intermediate variable:

```
unsigned long myValue = 2;
unsigned long cubed   = cube(myValue);      // cubed = 8
unsigned long squared = square(cubed);      // squared = 64
unsigned long tripled = triple(squared);    // tripled = 192
unsigned long Answer  = double(tripled);    // Answer = 384
```

Now each intermediate result can be examined, and the order of execution is explicit.

PARAMETERS ARE LOCAL VARIABLES

The arguments passed in to the function are local to the function. Changes made to the arguments do not affect the values in the calling function. This is known as *passing by value*, which means a local copy of each argument is made in the function. These local copies are treated just like any other local variables. Listing 6.1 illustrates this point.

LISTING **6.1**   DEMONSTRATES PASSING BY VALUE

```
1:      // Listing 6.1 - demonstrates passing by value
2:
3:      #include <iostream.h>
4:
5:      void swap(int x, int y);
6:
7:      int main()
8:      {
9:         int x = 5, y = 10;
10:
11:        cout << " Main. Before swap, x: "  ;
12:        cout << x << "  y: "  << y << " \n" ;
13:        swap(x,y);
14:        cout << " Main. After swap, x: "  << x ;
15:          cout << "  y: "  << y << " \n" ;
16:        return 0;
17:     }
18:
19:     void swap (int x, int y)
20:     {
21:        int temp;
22:
23:        cout << " Swap. Before swap, x: ";
24:          cout << x << "  y: "  << y << " \n" ;
25:
26:        temp = x;
27:        x = y;
28:        y = temp;
29:
30:        cout << " Swap. After swap, x: ";
31:          cout << x << "  y: "  << y << " \n" ;
32:
33:     }
```

```
Main. Before swap. x: 5 y: 10
Swap. Before swap. x: 5 y: 10
Swap. After swap. x: 10 y: 5
Main. After swap. x: 5 y: 10
```

This program initializes two variables in main() and then passes them to the swap() function, which appears to swap them. When they are examined again in main(), however, they are unchanged!

The variables are initialized on line 9, and their values are displayed on line 11. swap() is called, and the variables are passed in.

Execution of the program switches to the swap() function, where on line 21 the values are printed again. They are in the same order as they were in main(), as expected. On lines 23–25, the values are swapped, and this action is confirmed by the printout on line 27. Indeed, while in the swap() function, the values are swapped.

Execution then returns to line 13, back in main(), where the values are no longer swapped.

As you've figured out, the values passed into the swap() function are passed by value, meaning that copies of the values are made that are local to swap(). These local variables are swapped in lines 23–25, but the variables back in main() are unaffected.

Later in the book, you'll see alternatives to passing by value that will allow the values in main() to be changed.

RETURN VALUES

Functions return a value or return void. void is a signal to the compiler that no value will be returned.

To return a value from a function, write the keyword return followed by the value you want to return. The value might itself be an expression that returns a value. For example

```
return 5;
return (x > 5);
return (MyFunction());
```

These are all legal return statements, assuming that the function MyFunction() itself returns a value. The value in the second statement, `return (x > 5)`, will be zero if x is not greater than 5, or it will be 1. What is returned is the value of the expression, false or true, not the value of x.

When the `return` keyword is encountered, the expression following `return` is returned as the value of the function. Program execution returns immediately to the calling function, and any statements following the return are not executed.

It is legal to have more than one `return` statement in a single function. However, keep in mind that as soon as a return statement is executed, the function ends.

DEFAULT PARAMETERS

For every parameter you declare in a function prototype and definition, the calling function must pass in a value, unless you define a default value. A default value is a value to use if none is supplied. Thus you can write

```
long myFunction (int x = 50);
```

This prototype says, "`myFunction()` returns a `long` and takes an integer parameter. If an argument is not supplied, use the default value of 50."

The function definition is not changed by declaring a default parameter. The function definition header for this function would be

```
long myFunction (int x)
```

If the calling function did not include a parameter, the compiler would fill x with the default value of 50.

Any or all the function's parameters can be assigned default values. The one restriction is this: If any parameter has a default value, all following parameters must also have default values.

If the function prototype looks like

```
long myFunction (int Param1, int
➥Param2, int Param3);
```

you can assign a default value to Param2 only if you have assigned a default value to Param3. You can assign a default value to Param1 only if you've assigned default values to both Param2 and Param3.

OVERLOADING FUNCTIONS

C++ enables you to create more than one function with the same name. This is called function overloading. The functions must differ in their parameter list, with a different type of parameter, a different number of parameters, or both. Here's an example:

```
int myFunction (int, int);
int myFunction (long, long);
int myFunction (long);
```

myFunction() is overloaded with three different parameter lists. The first and second versions differ in the types of the parameters, and the third differs in the number of parameters. This is a useful technique, which allows you to call myFunction() and pass in any matching parameter list, without having to remember three different function names.

The return types can be the same or different on overloaded functions, as long as the parameter list is different. You can't overload just on return type, however.

In this lesson, you learned how to declare and define functions and how to pass in parameters. You also learned how to return values from functions and how to overload functions.

LESSON 7
CLASSES

In this lesson, you will learn what classes and objects are and how to define a new class and create objects of that class. Classes extend the built-in capabilities of C++ to assist you in representing and solving complex, real-world problems.

CREATING NEW TYPES

The type of a variable tells you its size and also the capabilities of the object. For example, integers can be added together. Thus, just by declaring `Height` and `Width` to be integers, you know that it is possible to add `Height` to `Width` and to assign that number to another number.

A *type* is a category. Familiar types include car, house, person, and shape. In C++, a type is an object with a size, a state, and a set of abilities.

A C++ programmer can create any type needed, and each of these new types can have all the functionality and power of the built-in types.

WHY CREATE A NEW TYPE?

Programs are usually written to solve real-world problems, such as keeping track of employee records or simulating the workings of a heating system. Although it is possible to solve these problems by using programs written with only integers and characters, it is far easier if you can create representations of the objects that you are talking about. In other words, simulating the workings of a heating system is easier if you can create variables that represent rooms, heat sensors, thermostats, and boilers. The closer these variables correspond to reality, the easier it is to write the program.

CLASSES AND MEMBERS

You make a new type by declaring a class. A *class* is just a collection of variables—often of different types—combined with a set of related functions.

Clients of your class are other classes or functions that make use of your class. *Encapsulation* allows the clients of your class to use it without knowing or caring about how it works. They only need to know what it does, not how it does it.

 Encapsulation   The bundling together of all the information, capabilities, and responsibilities of an entity into a single object.

A class can consist of any combination of the variable types and also other class types. The variables in the class are referred to as the *member variables* or *data members*.

The functions in the class typically manipulate the member variables. They are referred to as *member functions* or *methods* of the class.

DECLARING A CLASS

To declare a class, you use the `class` keyword followed by an opening brace and then list the data members and methods of that class. End the declaration with a closing brace and a semicolon. Here's the declaration of a class called `Cat`:

```
class Cat
{
public:
    unsigned int  itsAge;
    unsigned int  itsWeight;
    Meow();
};
```

Declaring this class doesn't allocate memory for a `Cat`. It just tells the compiler what a `Cat` is, what data it contains (`itsAge` and `itsWeight`), and what it can do (`Meow()`). It also tells the compiler how big a `Cat` is—that is, how much room the compiler must set aside for each `Cat` that you create. In this example, if an integer is 4 bytes, a Cat is only 8 bytes big: itsAge is 4 bytes, and itsWeight is another 4. Meow() takes up no room because no storage space is set aside for member functions (methods).

DEFINING AN OBJECT

You define an object of your new type just as you define an integer variable:

```
unsigned int GrossWeight;      // define an unsigned integer
Cat Frisky;                    // define a Cat
```

An object is simply an individual instance of a class.

ACCESSING CLASS MEMBERS

Once you define an actual Cat object (for example, Frisky), you use the dot operator (.) to access the members of that object. Therefore, to assign 50 to Frisky's itsWeight member variable, you would write

```
Frisky.itsWeight = 50;
```

In the same way, to call the Meow() function, you would write

```
Frisky.Meow();
```

PRIVATE VERSUS PUBLIC

Other keywords are used in the declaration of a class. Two of the most important are public and private.

All members of a class—data and methods—are private by default. Private members can be accessed only within methods of the class itself. Public members can be accessed through any object of the class. This distinction is both important and confusing. To make it a bit clearer, consider an example from earlier in this chapter:

```
class Cat
{
    unsigned int  itsAge;
    unsigned int  itsWeight;
    Meow();
};
```

In this declaration, `itsAge`, `itsWeight`, and `Meow()` are all private, because all members of a class are private by default. This means that unless you specify otherwise, they are private.

However, if you write

```
Cat  Boots;
Boots.itsAge=5;    // error! can't access private data!
```

the compiler flags this as an error. In effect, you've said to the compiler, "I'll access `itsAge`, `itsWeight`, and `Meow()` from only within member functions of the `Cat` class." Yet here you've accessed it from outside a `Cat` method. Just because `Boots` is an object of class `Cat`, that doesn't mean that you can access the parts of `Boots` that are private.

The way to use `Cat` so that you can access the data members is to declare a section of the `Cat` declaration to be public:

```
class Cat
{
public:
    unsigned int  itsAge;
    unsigned int  itsWeight;
    Meow();
};
```

Now `itsAge`, `itsWeight`, and `Meow()` are all public. `Boots.itsAge=5` compiles without a problem.

MAKE MEMBER DATA PRIVATE

As a general rule of design, you should keep the member data of a class private and write public methods to *set* and *get* their value. These methods are often called *accessor* methods.

IMPLEMENTING CLASS METHODS

Every class method that you declare must also be defined.

A member *function definition* begins with the name of the class followed by two colons, the name of the function, and its parameters. Listing 7.1 shows the complete declaration of a simple `Cat` class and the implementation of its accessor function and one general class member function.

LISTING 7.1   IMPLEMENTING THE METHODS OF A SIMPLE CLASS

```
1:   // Demonstrates declaration of a class and
2:   // definition of class methods,
3:
4:   #include <iostream.h>      // for cout
5:
6:   class Cat              // begin declaration of the class
7:   {
8:   public:                    // begin public section
9:       int GetAge();          // accessor function
10:      void SetAge (int age); // accessor function
11:      void Meow();           // general function
12:  private:                   // begin private section
13:      int itsAge;            // member variable
14:  };
15:
16:  // GetAge, Public accessor function
17:  // returns value of itsAge member
18:  int Cat::GetAge()
19:  {
20:      return itsAge;
21:  }
22:
23:  // definition of SetAge, public
24:  // accessor function
25:  // returns sets itsAge member
26:  void Cat::SetAge(int age)
27:  {
28:      // set member variable its age to
29:      // value passed in by parameter age
30:      itsAge = age;
31:  }
32:
33:  // definition of Meow method
34:  // returns: void
35:  // parameters: None
36:  // action: Prints "meow" to screen
37:  void Cat::Meow()
38:  {
39:      cout << "Meow.\n";
40:  }
41:
42:  // create a cat, set its age, have it
43:  // meow, tell us its age, then meow again.
44:  int main()
45:  {
```

continues

LISTING 7.1   CONTINUED

```
46:        Cat Frisky;
47:        Frisky.SetAge(5);
48:        Frisky.Meow();
49:        cout << "Frisky is a cat who is " ;
50:        cout << Frisky.GetAge() << " years old.\n";
51:        Frisky.Meow();
52;        return 0;
53:    }
```

OUTPUT

```
Meow.
Frisky is a cat who is 5 years old.
Meow.
```

Lines 6–14 contain the definition of the Cat class. Line 8 contains the keyword public, which tells the compiler that what follows is a set of public members. Line 9 has the declaration of the public accessor method GetAge(). GetAge() provides access to the private member variable itsAge, which is declared in line 13. Line 10 has the public accessor function SetAge(). SetAge() takes an integer as an argument and sets itsAge to the value of that argument.

Line 12 begins the private section, which includes only the declaration in line 13 of the private member variable itsAge. The class declaration ends with a closing brace and semicolon in line 14.

Lines 18–21 contain the definition of the member function GetAge(). This method takes no parameters; it returns an integer. Note that class methods include the class name followed by two colons and the function's name (line 18). This syntax tells the compiler that the GetAge() function you are defining here is the one that you declared in the Cat class. With the exception of this header line, the GetAge() function is created like any other function.

The GetAge() function takes only one line; it returns the value in itsAge. Note that the main() function cannot access itsAge because itsAge is private to the Cat class. The main() function has access to the public method GetAge(). Because GetAge() is a member function of the Cat class, it has full access to the itsAge variable. This access enables GetAge() to return the value of itsAge to main().

Lines 26–31 contain the definition of the SetAge() member function. It takes an integer parameter and sets the value of itsAge to the value of that parameter in line 30. Because it is a member of the Cat class, SetAge() has direct access to the member variable itsAge.

Line 37 begins the definition, or implementation, of the Meow() method of the Cat class. It is a one-line function that prints the word Meow to the screen, followed by a new line. (Remember that the \n character prints a new line to the screen.)

Line 44 begins the body of the program with the familiar main() function. In this case, it takes no arguments and returns int. In line 46, main() declares a Cat named Frisky. In line 47, the value 5 is assigned to the itsAge member variable by way of the SetAge() accessor method. Note that the method is called by using the class name (Frisky) followed by the member operator (.) and the method name (SetAge()). In this same way, you can call any of the other methods in a class.

Line 48 calls the Meow() member function, and lines 49 and 50 print a message using the GetAge() accessor. Line 51 calls Meow() again.

In this lesson, you learned what classes and objects are and how to define a new class and create objects of that class.

LESSON 8

MORE ABOUT CLASSES

In this lesson, you will learn how to initialize the state of your classes using constructors and how to make member methods constant. Classes have methods which provide their capabilities, and they have variables which provide their state.

CONSTRUCTORS AND DESTRUCTORS

There are two ways to define an integer variable. You can define the variable and then assign a value to it later in the program. For example:

```
int Weight;          // define a variable
...                  // other code here
Weight = 7;          // assign it a value
```

Or you can define the integer and immediately initialize it. For example:

```
int Weight = 7;      // define and initialize to 7
```

Initialization combines the definition of the variable with its initial assignment. Nothing stops you from changing that value later. Initialization ensures that your variable is never without a meaningful value.

How do you initialize the member data of a class? Classes have a special member function called a *constructor*. The constructor can take parameters as needed, but it cannot have a return value—not even void. The constructor is a class method with the same name as the class itself.

Whenever you declare a constructor, you'll also want to declare a *destructor*. Just as constructors create and initialize objects of your class, destructors clean up after your object and free any memory you might have allocated. A destructor always has the name of the class preceded by a tilde (~). Destructors take no arguments and have no return value. Therefore, the Cat declaration includes

```
~Cat();
```

DEFAULT CONSTRUCTORS

When you write

```
Cat Frisky(5);
```

you invoke the constructor for Cat that takes one parameter (in this case, the value 5). If, however, you write

```
Cat Frisky;
```

the compiler allows you to leave the parentheses off and calls the *default constructor*.

Default Constructor   The constructor that takes no parameters.

CONSTRUCTORS PROVIDED BY THE COMPILER

If you declare no constructors at all, the compiler will create a default constructor for you. (Remember, the default constructor is the constructor that takes no parameters.)

The default constructor the compiler provides takes no action; it is as if you had declared a constructor that took no parameters and whose body was empty.

There are two important points to note about this:

- The default constructor is any constructor that takes no parameters, whether you declare it or you get it for free from the compiler.

- If you declare any constructor (with or without parameters), the compiler will not provide a default constructor for you. In that case, if you want a default constructor, you must declare it yourself.

If you fail to declare a destructor, the compiler will also give you one of those, and this, too, will have an empty body and will do nothing.

As a matter of form, if you declare a constructor, be sure to declare a
destructor, even if your destructor does nothing. Although it is true that
the default destructor would work correctly, it doesn't hurt to declare your
own, and it makes your code clearer.

Listing 8.1 rewrites the Cat class to use a constructor to initialize the Cat
object, setting its age to whatever initial age you provide. It also demonstrates where the destructor is called.

LISTING 8.1   USING CONSTRUCTORS AND DESTRUCTORS

```
1:    // Demonstrates declaration of a constructor and
2:    // destructor for the Cat class
3:
4:    #include <iostream.h>        // for cout
5:
6:    class Cat                    // begin declaration of the class
7:    {
8:      public:                    // begin public section
9:        Cat(int initialAge);     // constructor
10:       ~Cat();                  // destructor
11:       int GetAge();            // accessor function
12:       void SetAge(int age);    // accessor function
13:       void Meow();
14:     private:                   // begin private section
15:       int itsAge;              // member variable
16:    };
17:
18:    // constructor of Cat,
19:    Cat::Cat(int initialAge)
20:    {
21:        itsAge = initialAge;
22:    }
23:
24:    Cat::~Cat()                  // destructor, takes no action
25:    {
26:    }
27:
28:    // GetAge, Public accessor function
29:    // returns value of itsAge member
30:    int Cat::GetAge()
31:    {
32:        return itsAge;
33:    }
34:
```

```
35:    // Definition of SetAge, public
36:    // accessor function
37:
38:    void Cat::SetAge(int age)
39:    {
40:        // set member variable itsAge to
41:        // value passed in by parameter age
42:        itsAge = age;
43:    }
44:
45:    // definition of Meow method
46:    // returns: void
47:    // parameters: None
48:    // action: Prints "meow" to screen
49:    void Cat::Meow()
50:    {
51:        cout << "Meow.\n";
52:    }
53:
54:    // create a cat, set its age, have it
55:    // meow, tell us its age, then meow again.
56:    int main()
57:    {
58:       Cat Frisky(5);
59:       Frisky.Meow();
60:       cout << "Frisky is a cat who is " ;
61:       cout << Frisky.GetAge() << " years old.\n";
62:       Frisky.Meow();
63:       Frisky.SetAge(7);
64:       cout << "Now Frisky is " ;
65:       oout << Frisky.GetAge() << " years old.\n";
66;       return 0;
67: }
```

```
Meow,
Frisky is a cat who is 5 years old.
Meow.
Now Frisky is 7 years old.
```

On line 9 is a constructor that takes an integer. Line 10 declares the destructor, which takes no parameters. Destructors never take parameters, and neither constructors nor destructors return a value—not even void.

Lines 19–22 show the implementation of the constructor, which is similar to the implementation of the SetAge() accessor function. There is no return value.

Lines 24–26 show the implementation of the destructor ~Cat(). This function does nothing, but you must include the definition of the function if you declare it in the class declaration.

Line 58 contains the definition of a Cat object, Frisky. The value 5 is passed in to Frisky's constructor. There is no need to call SetAge(), because Frisky was created with the value 5 in its member variable itsAge, as shown in line 61. In line 63, Frisky's itsAge variable is reassigned to 7. Line 65 prints the new value.

const MEMBER FUNCTIONS

If you declare a class member function to be const, you are promising that the method won't change the value of any of the members of the class. To declare a class method as constant, put the keyword const after the parentheses but before the semicolon. The declaration of the *constant member function* SomeFunction() takes no arguments and returns void. It looks like this:

```
void SomeFunction() const;
```

Accessor functions are often declared as constant functions by using the const modifier. The Cat class has two accessor functions:

```
void SetAge(int anAge);
int GetAge();
```

SetAge() cannot be const because it changes the member variable itsAge. GetAge(), on the other hand, can and should be const because it doesn't change the class at all. It simply returns the current value of the member variable itsAge. Therefore, the declaration of these functions should be written like this:

```
void SetAge(int anAge);
int GetAge() const;
```

If you declare a function to be const and then the implementation of that function changes the object (by changing the value of any of its members), the compiler will flag it as an error. For example, if you wrote GetAge() in such a way that it kept count of the number of times that the Cat was asked its age, it would generate a compiler error. This is because you would be changing the Cat object by calling this method.

Use const Often   Use const whenever possible.
Declare member functions to be const whenever they
should not change the object. This lets the compiler
help you find errors; it's faster and less expensive than
doing it yourself.

It is good programming practice to declare as many methods to be const
as possible. Each time you do, you enable the compiler to catch your
errors, instead of letting your errors become bugs that will show up when
your program is running.

In this lesson, you learned how to initialize the state of your classes using
constructors and how to make member methods constant.

LESSON 9
USING CLASSES WELL

In this lesson, you'll learn how to manage your classes and how to enlist the compiler in helping you find and avoid bugs. Classes are the key concept in C++.

INTERFACE VERSUS IMPLEMENTATION

Clients are the parts of the program that create and use objects of your class. Your class's interface declaration is a contract with these clients. The contract tells what data your class has available and how your class will behave.

Errors at Different Programming Stages Compile-time errors—that is, errors found while you are compiling—are far better than runtime errors—that is, errors found while you are executing the program.

Compile-time errors can be found much more reliably. It is possible to run a program many times without going down every possible code path. Therefore, a runtime error can hide for quite some time. Compile-time errors are found every time you compile, so they are easier to identify and fix. It is the goal of quality programming to ensure that the code has no runtime bugs. One tried-and-true technique is to use the compiler to catch your mistakes early in the development process.

Of course, your code can be perfectly legal but not do what you intend. That is why you still need a quality assurance team.

WHERE TO PUT CLASS DECLARATIONS AND METHOD DEFINITIONS

Each function you declare for your class must have a definition in a file the compiler can find, typically a file whose name ends with .cpp. If you are using the Microsoft compiler, you will add this file to your project. Other compilers use make files or project files to keep track of which files must be compiled.

Use the .CPP extension   Many compilers assume that files ending with .C are C programs, and that C++ program files end with .CPP. You can use any extension, but .CPP will minimize confusion.

PUT CLASS DECLARATIONS IN HEADER FILES

The declaration of a class tells the compiler what the class is, what data it holds, and what functions it has. The declaration of the class is called its interface because it tells the user how to interact with the class. The interface is usually stored in an .HPP file, which is referred to as a header file.

The function definition tells the compiler how the function works. The function definition is called the *implementation* of the class method, and it is kept in a .CPP file.

For example, I put the declaration of the Cat class into a file named CAT.HPP, and I put the definition of the class methods into a file called CAT.CPP. I then incorporate the header file into the .CPP file by putting the following code at the top of CAT.CPP:

```
#include "Cat.hpp"
```

This tells the compiler to read CAT.HPP into the file, just as if I had typed in its contents at this point. Why bother separating them if you're just going to read them back in? Most of the time, clients of your class don't care about the implementation specifics. Reading the header file tells them everything they need to know; they can ignore the implementation files.

INLINE IMPLEMENTATION

When you call a function, execution of the program jumps to that function and then returns when the function exits. This jumping takes time; an alternative is to declare the function inline. When you declare a function inline, the compiler makes a copy of the entire function right in the place you call it. This saves time but increases the size of your code.

To make a member function inline, put the keyword `inline` before the return value of the member function. The inline implementation of the `GetWeight()` function, for example, looks like this:

```
inline int Cat::GetWeight()
{
    return itsWeight;        // return the Weight data member
}
```

You can also put the definition of a function into the declaration of the class, automatically making that function inline. The following is an example:

```
class Cat
{
public:etWeight() const { return itsWeight; }    // inline
    void SetWeight(int aWeight);
private:
    int itsWeight;
};
```

 Do Not Use Inline Functions   The compiler is better at optimizing your code than you think. Avoid using inline functions; let the compiler make your code run as fast as it can.

CLASSES WITH OTHER CLASSES AS MEMBER DATA

It is not uncommon to build up a complex class by declaring simpler classes and including them in the declaration of the more complicated class. For example, you might declare a `Wheel` class, a `Motor` class, a

Transmission class, and so forth, and then combine them into a Car class. This declares a *has-a* relationship: A car has a motor, it has wheels, and it has a transmission.

Consider a second example. A rectangle is composed of lines. A line is defined by two points. A point is defined by an x coordinate and a y coordinate. Listing 9.1 shows a complete declaration of a Rectangle class as it might appear in RECTANGLE.HPP. Because a rectangle is defined as four lines connecting four points, and each point refers to a coordinate on a graph, a Point class is first declared to hold the x,y coordinates of each point. Listing 9.1 shows a complete declaration of both classes.

LISTING 9.1   DECLARING A COMPLETE CLASS

```
1:    // Begin Rect.hpp
2:    #include <iostream.h>
3:    class Point        // holds x,y coordinates
4:    {
5:        // no constructor, use default
6:        public:
7:            void SetX(int x) { itsX = x; }
8:            void SetY(int y) { itsY = y; }
9:            int GetX()const { return itsX;}
10:           int GetY()const { return itsY;}
11:       private:
12:           int itsX;
13:           int itsY;
14:   };     // end of Point class declaration
15:
16:
17: class   Rectangle
18: {
19: public:
20:    Rectangle (int top, int left,
          ➥int bottom, int right);
21:    ~Rectangle () {}
22:
23:    int GetTop() const { return itsTop; }
24:    int GetLeft() const { return itsLeft; }
25:    int GetBottom() const { return itsBottom; }
26:    int GetRight() const { return itsRight; }
27:
28:    Point  GetUpperLeft() const
          ➥{ return itsUpperLeft; }
29:    Point  GetLowerLeft() const
```

continues

LISTING 9.1   CONTINUED

```
      ➥{ return itsLowerLeft; }
30:    Point  GetUpperRight() const
      ➥{ return itsUpperRight; }
31:    Point  GetLowerRight() const
      ➥{ return itsLowerRight; }
32:
33:    void SetUpperLeft(Point Location)
      ➥{itsUpperLeft = Location;}
34:    void SetLowerLeft(Point Location)
      ➥{itsLowerLeft = Location;}
35:    void SetUpperRight(Point Location)
      ➥{itsUpperRight = Location;}
36:    void SetLowerRight(Point Location)
      ➥{itsLowerRight = Location;}37:
38:    void SetTop(int top) { itsTop = top; }
39:    void SetLeft (int left) { itsLeft = left; }
40:    void SetBottom (int bottom)
      ➥{ itsBottom = bottom; }
41:    void SetRight (int right) { itsRight = right; }
42:
43:    int GetArea() const;
44:
45:      private:
46:          Point  itsUpperLeft;
47:          Point  itsUpperRight;
48:          Point  itsLowerLeft;
49:          Point  itsLowerRight;
50:          int    itsTop;
51:          int    itsLeft;
52:          int    itsBottom;
53:          int    itsRight;
54:    };
55:    // end Rect.hpp
```

LISTING 9.2   RECT.CPP

```
1:    // Begin rect.cpp
2:    #include ""rect.hpp"
3:    Rectangle::Rectangle
      ➥(int top, int left, int bottom, int right)
4:    {
5:          itsTop = top;
6:          itsLeft = left;
7:          itsBottom = bottom;
8:          itsRight = right;
9:
```

```
10:             itsUpperLeft.SetX(left);
11:             itsUpperLeft.SetY(top);
12:
13:             itsUpperRight.SetX(right);
14:             itsUpperRight.SetY(top);
15:
16:             itsLowerLeft.SetX(left);
17:             itsLowerLeft.SetY(bottom);
18:
19:             itsLowerRight.SetX(right);
20:             itsLowerRight.SetY(bottom);
21:   }
22:
23:
24:   // compute area of the rectangle by finding corners,
25:   // establish width and height and then multiply
26:   int Rectangle::GetArea() const
27:   {
28:             int Width = itsRight - itsLeft;
29:             int Height = itsTop - itsBottom;
30:             return (Width * Height);
31:   }
32:
33:   int main()
34:   {
35:             //initialize a local Rectangle variable
36:             Rectangle MyRectangle (100, 20, 50, 80 );
37:
38:             int Area = MyRectangle.GetArea();
39:
40:             cout << ""Area: " << Area << "\n";
41:             cout << "Upper Left X Coordinate: ";
42:             cout << MyRectangle.GetUpperLeft().GetX();
43:          return 0;
44:   }
```

```
Area: 3000
Upper Left X Coordinate: 20
```

Lines 3–14 in Listing 9.1 declare the class Point, which is used to hold a specific x,y coordinate on a graph. As written, this program doesn't use Points much. However, other drawing methods require Points.

Within the declaration of the class Point, you declare two member variables—itsX and itsY—on lines 12 and 13. These variables hold the values of the coordinates. As the x coordinate increases, you move to the right on the graph. As the y coordinate increases, you move upward on the graph. Other graphs use different systems. Some windowing programs, for example, increase the y coordinate as you move down in the window.

The Point class uses inline accessor functions to get and set the X and Y points declared on lines 7–10. Points use the default constructor and destructor; therefore, you must set their coordinates explicitly.

Line 17 begins the declaration of a Rectangle class. A Rectangle consists of four points that represent the corners of the Rectangle.

The constructor for the Rectangle (line 20) takes four integers, known as top, left, bottom, and right. The four parameters to the constructor are copied into four member variables, and then the four Points are established.

In addition to the usual accessor functions, Rectangle has a function named GetArea() declared in line 43. Instead of storing the area as a variable, the GetArea() function computes the area on lines 28–30 of Listing 9.2. To do this, it computes the width and the height of the rectangle and then multiplies those two values.

Getting the x coordinate of the upper-left corner of the rectangle requires that you access the UpperLeft point and ask that point for its X value. Because GetUpperLeft()is a method of Rectangle, it can directly access the private data of Rectangle, including itsUpperLeft. Because itsUpperLeft is a Point, and Point's itsX value is private, GetUpperLeft() cannot directly access this data. Rather, it must use the public accessor function GetX() to obtain that value.

Line 33 of Listing 9.2 is the beginning of the body of the actual program. Until line 36, no memory has been allocated, and nothing has really happened. The only thing I've done is to tell the compiler how to make a Point and how to make a Rectangle, in case one is ever needed.

In line 36, I define a Rectangle by passing in values for top, left, bottom, and right.

In line 38, I make a local variable, Area, of type int. This variable holds the area of the Rectangle that I've created. Area is initialized with the value returned by Rectangle's GetArea() function.

A client of Rectangle could create a Rectangle object and get its area without ever looking at the implementation of GetArea().

Just by looking at the header file, which contains the declaration of the Rectangle class, the programmer knows that GetArea() returns an int. How GetArea() does its magic is not of concern to the user of class Rectangle. In fact, the author of Rectangle could change GetArea() without affecting the programs that use the Rectangle class.

In this lesson, you learned how to distinguish interface from implementation and how to build complex classes out of simpler classes.

LESSON 10
LOOPING

In this lesson, you will learn about while *loops,* do-while *loops and* for *loops.*

LOOPING

Many programming problems are solved by repeatedly acting on the same data. This process is called *iteration*.

 Iteration Doing the same thing again and again. The principal method of iteration is the loop.

while LOOPS

A while loop causes your program to repeat a sequence of statements as long as the starting condition remains true.

The condition tested by a while loop can be as complex as any legal C++ expression. This can include expressions produced using the logical && (and), ¦¦ (or), and ! (not) operators.

continue AND break

At times, you'll want to return to the top of a while loop before the entire set of statements in the while loop is executed. The continue statement jumps back to the top of the loop.

At other times, you might want to exit the loop before the exit conditions are met. The break statement immediately exits the while loop, and program execution resumes after the closing brace.

Listing 10.1 demonstrates the use of these statements. This program is a game. The user is invited to enter a small number, a large number, a skip number, and a target number. The small number will be incremented by 1, and the large number will be decremented by 2. The decrement will be skipped each time the small number is a multiple of the skip. The game ends if small becomes larger than large. If the large number reaches the target exactly, a statement is printed and the game stops.

The user's goal is to put in a target number for the large number that will stop the game.

LISTING 10.1 while LOOPS

```
1:      // Listing 10.1
2:      // Demonstrates a while loop
3:
4:      #include <iostream.h>
5:
6:      int main()
7:      {
8:          unsigned short small;
9:          unsigned long   large;
10:         unsigned long   skip;
11:         unsigned long target;
12:         const unsigned short MAXSMALL=65535;
13:
14:         cout << "Enter a small number: ";
15:         cin >> small;
16:         cout << "Enter a large number: ";
17:         cin >> large;
18:         cout << "Enter a skip number: ";
19:         cin >> skip;
20:         cout << "Enter a target number: ";
21:         cin >> target;
22:
23:         cout << "\n";
24:
25:         // set up 3 stop conditions for the loop
26:         while (small < large && large >
        ➥0 && small < MAXSMALL)
27:
28:         {
29:
30:             small++;
```

continues

LISTING 10.1 CONTINUED

```
31:
32:            if (small % skip == 0)  // skip the decrement?
33:            {
34:               cout << "skipping on " << small << endl;
35:               continue;
36:            }
37:
38:            if (large == target) // exact match for the target?
39:            {
40:               cout << "Target reached!";
41:               break;
42:            }
43:
44:            large-=2;
45:         }                        // end of while loop
46:
47:         cout << "\nSmall: " << small << " Large: " ;
48:         cout << large << endl;
49:         return 0;
50:     }
```

```
Enter a small number: 2
Enter a large number: 20
Enter a skip number: 4
Enter a target number: 6

skipping on 4
skipping on 8

Small: 10 Large: 8
```

In this play, the user lost; small became larger than large before the
target number of 6 was reached.

On line 26, the while conditions are tested. If small continues to be
smaller than large, large is larger than 0, and small hasn't overrun the
maximum value for an unsigned short int, the body of the while loop is
entered.

On line 32, the small value is taken modulo the skip value. If small is a
multiple of skip, the continue statement is reached and program execution jumps to the top of the loop at line 26. This effectively skips over the
test for the target and the decrement of large.

On line 38, target is tested against the value for large. If they are the same, the user has won. A message is printed and the `break` statement is reached. This causes an immediate break out of the `while` loop, and program execution resumes on line 46.

Both `continue` and `break` should be used with caution. They are the next most dangerous commands after `goto`, for much the same reason. Programs that suddenly change direction are difficult to understand, and liberal use of `continue` and `break` can render even a small `while` loop unreadable.

`do...while` LOOPS

It is possible that the body of a `while` loop will never execute. The `while` statement checks its condition before executing any of its statements, and if the condition evaluates `false`, the entire body of the `while` loop is skipped.

An alternative is to use a `do...while` loop which executes the body of the loop before its condition is tested and ensures that the body always executes at least one time. Listing 10.2 demonstrates.

LISTING 10.2   DEMONSTRATING A `do...while` LOOP

```
1:      // Listing 10.2
2:      // Demonstrates do while
3:
4:      #include <iostream.h>
5:
6:      int main()
7:      {
8:          int counter;
9:          cout << "How many hellos? ";
10:         cin >> counter;
11:         do
12:         {
13:             cout << "Hello\n";
14:             counter--;
15:         } while (counter >0 );
16:         cout << "counter is: " << counter << endl;
17:         return 0;
18:     }
```

```
How many hellos? 2
Hello
Hello
counter is: 0
```

The user is prompted for starting a value on line 9 that is stored in the integer variable counter. In the do...while loop, the body of the loop is entered before the condition is tested, and therefore, is guaranteed to be acted on at least once. On line 13 the message is printed, on line 14 the counter is decremented, and on line 15 the condition is tested. If the condition evaluates true, execution jumps to the top of the loop on line 13; otherwise it falls through to line 16.

The continue and break statements work in the do...while loop exactly as they do in the while loop. The only difference between a while loop and a do...while loop is when the condition is tested.

for LOOPS

When programming while loops, you'll often find yourself setting up a starting condition, testing to see if the condition is true, and incrementing or otherwise changing a variable each time through the loop.

A for loop combines the three steps of initialization, test, and incremention into one statement. A for statement consists of the keyword for followed by a pair of parentheses. Within the parentheses are three statements separated by semicolons.

The first statement is the initialization. Any legal C++ statement can be put here, but typically this is used to create and initialize a counting variable. Statement two is the test, and any legal C++ expression can be used there. This serves the same role as the condition in the while loop. Statement three is the action. Typically, a value is incremented or decremented, although any legal C++ statement can be put there.

Statements one and three can be any legal C++ statement, but statement two must be an expression—a C++ statement that returns a value. Listing 10.3 demonstrates the for loop.

LISTING **10.3** DEMONSTRATING THE **for** LOOP

```
1:      // Listing 10.3
2:      // Looping with for
3:
4:      #include <iostream.h>
5:
6:      int main()
7:      {
8:          int counter;
9:          for (counter = 0; counter < 5; counter++)
10:             cout << "Looping! ";
11:
12:         cout << "\nCounter: " << counter << ".\n";
13:         return 0;
14:     }
```

OUTPUT

```
Looping! Looping! Looping! Looping! Looping!
counter: 5.
```

The for statement on line 9 combines the initialization of counter, the test that counter is fewer than 5, and the increment of counter all into one line. The body of the for statement is on line 10. Of course, a block could be used here as well.

MULTIPLE INITIALIZATION AND INCREMENTS

It is not uncommon to initialize more than one variable, to test a compound logical expression, and to execute more than one statement. The initialization and action statements might be replaced by multiple C++ statements, each separated by a comma.

NULL STATEMENTS IN **for** LOOPS

Any or all the statements in a for loop can be null. To accomplish this, use the semicolon to mark where the statement would have been. To create a for loop that acts exactly like a while loop, leave out the first and third statement.

EMPTY **for** LOOPS

So much can be done in the header of a for statement that there are times you won't need the body to do anything at all. In that case, be sure to put a null statement (;) as the body of the loop. The semicolon can be on the same line as the header, but this is easy to overlook. Listing 10.4 illustrates how this is done.

LISTING **10.4**   ILLUSTRATING A NULL STATEMENT IN A for LOOP

```
1:      //Listing 10.4
2:      //Demonstrates null statement
3:      // as body of for loop
4:
5:      #include <iostream.h>
6:      int main()
7:      {
8:          for (int i = 0; i<5; cout << "i: "
            ➡<< i++ << endl)
9:              ;
10:         return 0;
11:     }
```

OUTPUT

```
i: 0
i: 1
i: 2
i: 3
i: 4
```

The for loop on line 8 includes three statements: the initialization statement establishes the counter i and initializes it to 0. The condition statement tests for i<5, and the action statement prints the value in i and increments it.

There is nothing left to do in the body of the for loop, so the null statement (;) is used. Note that this is not a well-designed for loop; the action statement is doing far too much. This would be better rewritten as

```
8:          for (int i = 0; i<5; i++)
9:              cout << "i: " << i << endl;
```

Although both do exactly the same thing, this example is easier to understand.

NESTED LOOPS

Loops can be nested, with one loop sitting in the body of another. The inner loop will be executed in full for every execution of the outer loop.

Listing 10.5 illustrates writing marks into a matrix using nested for loops.

LISTING 10.5 NESTED for LOOPS

```
1:    //Listing 10.5
2:    //Illustrates nested for loops
3:
4:    #include <iostream.h>
5:
6:    int main()
7:    {
8:         int rows, columns;
9:         char theChar;
10:        cout << "How many rows? ";
11:        cin >> rows;
12:        cout << "How many columns? ";
13:        cin >> columns;
14:        cout << "What character? ";
15:        cin >> theChar;
16:        for (int i = 0; i<rows; i++)
17:        {
18:             for (int j = 0; j<columns; j++)
19:                  cout << theChar;
20:             cout << "\n";
21:        }
22:        return 0;
23:    }
```

```
How many rows? 4
How many columns?   12
What character?   x
xxxxxxxxxxxx
xxxxxxxxxxxx
xxxxxxxxxxxx
xxxxxxxxxxxx
```

The user is prompted for the number of rows and columns and for a character to print. The first for loop, on line 16, initializes a counter (i) to 0, and then the body of the outer for loop is run.

On line 18, the first line of the body of the outer for loop, another for loop, is established. A second counter (j) is also initialized to 0, and the body of the inner for loop is executed. On line 19, the chosen character is printed, and control returns to the header of the inner for loop. Note that the inner for loop is only one statement (the printing of the character). The condition is tested (j < columns); if it evaluates to true, j is incremented and the next character is printed. This continues until j equals the number of columns.

When the inner for loop fails its test, in this case after 12 xs are printed, execution falls through to line 20, and a new line is printed. The outer for loop now returns to its header where its condition (i < rows) is tested. If this evaluates to true, i is incremented, and the body of the loop is executed.

In the second iteration of the outer for loop, the inner for loop is started over. Thus j is reinitialized to 0 (!) and the entire inner loop is run again.

The important idea here is that by using a nested loop, the inner loop is executed for each iteration of the outer loop. Thus the character is printed columns times for each row.

In this lesson you learned about while, do...while, and for loops.

LESSON 11

SWITCH STATEMENTS

In this lesson, you will learn about the switch *statement.*

switch STATEMENTS

if and else...if combinations can become quite confusing when nested too deeply, and C++ offers an alternative. Unlike if, which evaluates one value, switch statements enable you to branch on any of a number of different values. The general form of the switch statement is

```
switch (expression)
{
case valueOne: statement;
                    break;
case valueTwo: statement;
                    break;
....
case valueN:    statement;
                    break;
default:        statement;
}
```

expression is any legal C++ expression, and the statements are any legal C++ statements or block of statements. switch evaluates expression and compares the result to each of the case values.

 Evaluation for Equality   The evaluation is only for equality; relational operators cannot be used here, nor can Boolean operators.

If one of the case values matches the expression, execution jumps to those statements and continues to the end of the switch block unless a break statement is encountered. If nothing matches, execution branches to the optional default statement. If there is no default and there is no matching value, execution falls through the switch statement, and the statement ends.

 The default Case in switch Statements It is almost always a good idea to have a default case in switch statements. If you have no other need for the default, use it to test for the supposedly impossible case and print out an error message; this can be a tremendous aid in debugging.

It is important to note that if there is no break statement at the end of a case statement, execution will fall through to the next case. This is sometimes necessary, but usually is an error. If you decide to let execution fall through, be sure to put a comment indicating that you didn't just forget the break.

Listing 11.1 illustrates the use of the switch statement.

LISTING 11.1   DEMONSTRATING THE switch STATEMENT

```
1:  //Listing 11.1
2:  // Demonstrates switch statement
3:
4:  #include <iostream.h>
5:
6:  int main()
7:  {
8:      unsigned short int number;
9:      cout << "Enter a number between 1 and 5: ";
10:     cin >> number;
11:     switch (number)
12:     {
13:         case 0:   cout << "Too small, sorry!";
14:                   break;
15:         case 5:   cout << "Good job!\n";      // fall through
16:         case 4:   cout << "Nice Pick!\n";     // fall through
17:         case 3:   cout << "Excellent!\n";     // fall through
18:         case 2:   cout << "Masterful!\n";     // fall through
19:         case 1:   cout << "Incredible!\n";
20:                   break;
```

```
21:        default: cout << "Too large!\n";
22:                 break;
23:    }
24:    cout << "\n\n";
25:    return 0;
26: }
```

```
Enter a number between 1 and 5:  3
Excellent!
Masterful!
Incredible!

Enter a number between 1 and 5: 8
Too large!
```

> 💡 **A Note on the Output**   The output shown is the result of running this program twice.

The user is prompted for a number. That number is given to the switch statement. If the number is 0, the case statement on line 13 matches, the message Too small, sorry! is printed, and the break statement ends the switch. If the value is 5, execution switches to line 15 where a message is printed and then falls through to line 16, another message is printed, and so forth until hitting the break on line 20.

The net effect of these statements is that for a number between 1 and 5, many messages are printed. If the value of the number is not 0–5, it is assumed to be too large and the default statement is invoked on line 21.

In this lesson, you learned how and when to use the switch statement.

LESSON 12
POINTERS

In this lesson, you will learn what pointers are and how to declare and use pointers.

WHAT IS A POINTER?

One of the most powerful tools available to a C++ programmer is the capability to manipulate computer memory directly by using pointers. Pointers, however, are also considered one of the most confusing aspects of C++.

I believe pointers can be understood without confusion if you spend just a little time understanding what pointers really are.

A pointer is a variable that holds a memory address.

Stop. Read that again. A pointer is a variable. You know what a variable is; it is an object that can hold a value. An integer variable holds a number. A character variable holds a letter. A pointer is a variable that holds a memory address.

Okay, so what is a memory address? To fully understand this, you must know a little about computer memory. Don't panic; it isn't very difficult.

Computer memory is where these values are stored. By convention, computer memory is divided into sequentially numbered memory locations. Each of these locations is a memory address.

Every variable of every type is located at a unique location in address. Figure 12.1 shows a schematic representation of the storage of an unsigned long integer variable, theAge.

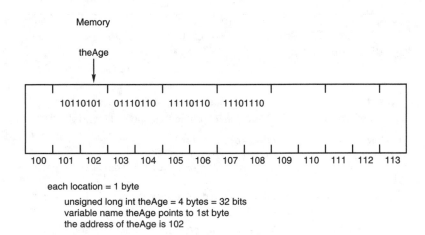

Memory

theAge

| | | | |
| 10110101 | 01110110 | 11110110 | 11101110 |

100   101   102   103   104   105   106   107   108   109   110   111   112   113

each location = 1 byte
unsigned long int theAge = 4 bytes = 32 bits
variable name theAge points to 1st byte
the address of theAge is 102

FIGURE 12.1   A schematic representation of theAge.

There is no reason why you would need to know the actual numeric value of the address of each variable. What you care about is that each one has an address, and that the right amount of memory is set aside.

How does the compiler know how much memory each variable needs? You tell the compiler how much memory to allow for your variables by declaring the variable type.

STORING THE ADDRESS IN A POINTER

Every variable has an address. Even without knowing the specific address of a given variable, you can store that address in a pointer.

For example, suppose that howOld is an integer. To declare a pointer called pAge to hold its address, you would write

```
int *pAge = 0;
```

This declares pAge to be a pointer to int. That is, pAge is declared to hold the address of an int.

In this example, pAge is initialized to 0. A pointer whose value is 0 is called a null pointer. All pointers, when they are created, should be initialized to something. If you don't know what you want to assign to the pointer, assign 0. A pointer that is not initialized is called a wild pointer. Wild pointers are very dangerous.

Be Safe   Practice safe computing: Initialize your pointers!

If you do initialize the pointer to 0, you must specifically assign the address of howOld to pAge. Here's an example that shows how to do that:

```
int howOld = 50;      // make a variable
int * pAge = 0;       // make a pointer
pAge = &howOld;               // put howOld's address in pAge
```

The first line creates a variable—howOld, whose type int—and initializes it with the value 50. The second line declares pAge to be a pointer to type int and initializes it to 0. You know that pAge is a pointer because of the asterisk (*) after the variable type and before the variable name.

The third and final line assigns the address of howOld to the pointer pAge. You can tell that the address of howOld is being assigned because of the address of operator (&).

At this point, pAge has as its value the address of howOld. howOld, in turn, has the value 50. You could have accomplished this with one fewer step, as in

```
int howOld = 50;       // make a variable
int * pAge = &howOld;  // make pointer to howOld
```

pAge is a pointer that now contains the address of the howOld variable. Using pAge, you can actually determine the value of howOld, which in this case is 50. Accessing howOld by using the pointer pAge is called indirection, because you are indirectly accessing howOld by means of pAge. Later today you will see how to use *indirection* to access a variable's value.

 Indirection   Accessing the value at the address held by a pointer. The pointer provides an indirect way to get the value held at that address.

POINTER NAMES

Pointers can have any name that is legal for other variables. This book follows the convention of naming all pointers with an initial p, as in pAge and pNumber.

THE INDIRECTION OPERATOR

The indirection operator (*) is also called the dereference operator. When a pointer is dereferenced, the value at the address stored by the pointer is retrieved.

MANIPULATING DATA BY USING POINTERS

After a pointer is assigned the address of a variable, you can use that pointer to access the data in that variable. Listing 12.1 demonstrates how the address of a local variable is assigned to a pointer and how the pointer manipulates the values in that variable.

LISTING 12.1   MANIPULATING DATA BY USING POINTERS

```
1:      // Listing 12.1 Using pointers
2:
3:      #include <iostream.h>
4:
5:
6:      int main()
7.      {
8:          int myAge;          // a variable
9:          int * pAge = 0;     // a pointer
10:         myAge = 5;
11:         cout << "myAge: " << myAge << "\n";
12:
13:         pAge = &myAge;      // assign address of myAge to pAge
14:
15:         cout << "*pAge: " << *pAge << "\n\n";
16:
17:         cout << "*pAge = 7\n";
18:
19:         *pAge = 7;          // sets myAge to 7
20:
21:         cout << "*pAge: " << *pAge << "\n";
22:         cout << "myAge: " << myAge << "\n\n";
23:
```

continues

LISTING 12.1   CONTINUED

```
24:
25:        cout << "myAge = 9\n";
26:
27:        myAge = 9;
28:
29:        cout << "myAge: " << myAge << "\n";
30:        cout << "*pAge: " << *pAge << "\n";
31:
32:        return 0;
33:    }
```

OUTPUT

```
myAge:  5
*pAge:  5

*pAge = 7
*pAge:  7
myAge:  7

myAge =9
myAge:  9
*pAge:  9
```

This program declares two variables: an int, myAge, and a pointer pAge, that is a pointer to int and holds the address of myAge. myAge, is assigned the value 5 in line 10; this is verified by the printout in line 11.

In line 13, pAge is assigned the address of myAge. In line 15, pAge is dereferenced and printed, showing that the value at the address that pAge stores is the 5 stored in myAge. In line 19, the value 7 is assigned to the variable at the address stored in pAge. This sets myAge to 7, and the printouts in lines 21–22 confirm this.

In line 27, the value 9 is assigned to the variable myAge. This value is obtained directly in line 29 and indirectly—by dereferencing pAge—in line 30.

WHY WOULD YOU USE POINTERS?

So far you've seen step-by-step details of assigning a variable's address to a pointer. In practice, though, you would never do this. After all, why bother with a pointer when you already have a variable with access to that value? The only reason for this kind of pointer manipulation of an automatic variable is to demonstrate how pointers work. Now that you are comfortable with the syntax of pointers, you can put them to good use.

THE STACK AND THE FREE STORE

Programmers generally deal with five areas of memory:

- Global name space
- The free store
- Registers
- Code space
- The stack

Local variables are on the stack, along with function parameters. Code is in code space, of course, and global variables are in global name space. The registers are used for internal housekeeping functions, such as keeping track of the top of the stack and the instruction pointer. Just about all remaining memory is given to the free store, that is sometimes referred to as the heap.

The problem with local variables is that they don't persist: When the function returns, the local variables are thrown away. Global variables solve that problem at the cost of unrestricted access throughout the program, that leads to the creation of code that is difficult to understand and maintain. Putting data in the free store solves both of these problems.

You can think of the free store as a massive section of memory where thousands of sequentially numbered cubbyholes lie waiting for your data. You can't label these cubbyholes, though, as you can with the stack. You must ask for the address of the cubbyhole you reserve and then stash that address away in a pointer.

One way to think about this is with an analogy: A friend gives you the 800 number for Acme Mail Order. You go home and program your telephone with that number, and then you throw away the piece of paper with the number on it. When you push the button, a telephone rings somewhere, and Acme Mail Order answers. You don't remember the number, and you don't know where the other telephone is located, but the button gives you access to Acme Mail Order. Acme Mail Order is your data on the free store. You don't know where it is, but you know how to get to it. You access it by using its address, in this case, the telephone number. You don't have to know that number; you just have to put it into a pointer— the button. The pointer gives you access to your data without bothering you with the details.

The stack is cleaned automatically when a function returns. All the local variables go out of scope, and they are removed from the stack. The free store is not cleaned until your program ends, and it is your responsibility to free any memory you've reserved when you are done with it. You want to be sure to free memory as soon as it is no longer needed to ensure that your program never runs out of memory; this is a good habit to develop early in your career.

The advantage to the free store is that the memory you reserve remains available until you explicitly free it. If you reserve memory on the free store while in a function, the memory is still available when the function returns.

The advantage of accessing memory in this way, rather than using global variables, is that only functions with access to the pointer have access to the data. This provides a tightly controlled interface to that data, and it eliminates the problem of one function changing that data in unexpected and unanticipated ways.

For this to work, you must be able to create a pointer to an area on the free store and to pass that pointer among functions. The following sections describe how to do this.

new

You allocate memory on the free store in C++ by using the new keyword. new is followed by the type of the object you want to allocate so the compiler knows how much memory is required. Therefore, new unsigned short int allocates 2 bytes in the free store, and new long allocates 4.

The return value from new is a memory address. It must be assigned to a pointer. To create an unsigned short on the free store, you might write

```
unsigned short int * pPointer;
pPointer = new unsigned short int;
```

You can, of course, initialize the pointer at its creation with

```
unsigned short int * pPointer = new
➥unsigned short int;
```

In either case, pPointer now points to an unsigned short int on the free store. You can use this like any other pointer to a variable and assign a value into that area of memory by writing

```
*pPointer = 72;
```

This means, "Put 72 at the value in pPointer," or "Assign the value 72 to the area on the free store to which pPointer points."

delete

When you are finished with your area of memory, you must call delete on the pointer. delete returns the memory to the free store. Remember that the pointer itself—as opposed to the memory to that it points—is a local variable. When the function where it is declared returns, that pointer goes out of scope and is lost. The memory allocated with the new operator is not freed automatically, but becomes unavailable—a situation called a memory leak. It's called a memory leak because that memory can't be recovered until the program ends. It is as though the memory has leaked out of your computer.

To restore the memory to the free store, you use the keyword delete. For example

```
delete pPointer;
```

When you delete the pointer, what you are really doing is freeing up the memory whose address is stored in the pointer. You are saying, "Return to the free store the memory that this pointer points to." The pointer is still a pointer, and it can be reassigned. Listing 12.2 demonstrates allocating a variable on the heap, using that variable, and deleting it.

Call delete on Null Pointers   When you call `delete` on a pointer, the memory it points to is freed. Calling `delete` on that pointer again will crash your program! When you delete a pointer, set it to 0 (null). Calling `delete` on a null pointer is guaranteed to be safe.

LISTING 12.2   ALLOCATING AND DELETING A POINTER

```
1:     // Listing 12.2
2:     // Allocating and deleting a pointer
3:
4:     #include <iostream.h>
5:     int main()
6:     {
7:         int localVariable = 5;
8:         int * pLocal= &localVariable;
9:         int * pHeap = new int;
10:        *pHeap = 7;
11:        cout << "localVariable: "
           ➥<< localVariable << "\n";
12:        cout << "*pLocal: " << *pLocal << "\n";
13:        cout << "*pHeap: " << *pHeap << "\n";
14:        delete pHeap;
15:        pHeap = new int;
16:        *pHeap = 9;
17:        cout << "*pHeap: " << *pHeap << "\n";
18:        delete pHeap;
19:        return 0;
20:    }
```

OUTPUT

```
localVariable: 5
*pLocal: 5
*pHeap: 7
*pHeap: 9
```

Line 7 declares and initializes a local variable. Line 8 declares and initializes a pointer with the address of the local variable. Line 9 declares another pointer but initializes it with the result obtained from calling `new int`. This allocates space on the free store for an `int`.

Line 10 assigns the value 7 to the newly allocated memory. Line 11 prints the value of the local variable, and line 12 prints the value pointed to by `pLocal`. As expected, these are the same. Line 18 prints the value pointed to by `pHeap`. It shows that the value assigned in line 10 is, in fact, accessible.

In line 14, the memory allocated in line 9 is returned to the free store by a call to delete. This frees the memory and disassociates the pointer from that memory. pHeap is now free to point to other memory. It is reassigned in lines 15 and 16, and line 17 prints the result. Line 18 restores that memory to the free store.

Although line 18 is redundant (the end of the program would have returned that memory), it is a good idea to free this memory explicitly. If the program changes or is extended, it will be beneficial that this step was already taken care of.

MEMORY LEAKS

Another way you might inadvertently create a memory leak is by reassigning your pointer before deleting the memory to which it points. Consider this code fragment

```
1:    unsigned short int * pPointer = new
      ➥unsigned short int;
2:    *pPointer = 72;
3:    pPointer = new unsigned short int;
4:    *pPointer = 84;
```

Line 1 creates pPointer and assigns it the address of an area on the free store. Line 2 stores the value 72 in that area of memory. Line 3 reassigns pPointer to another area of memory. Line 4 places the value 84 in that area. The original area—in which the value 72 is now held—is unavailable because the pointer to that area of memory has been reassigned. There is no way to access that original area of memory, nor is there any way to free it before the program ends.

The code should have been written like this:

```
1: unsigned short int * pPointer = new unsigned short int;
2: *pPointer = 72;
3: delete pPointer;
4: pPointer = new unsigned short int;
5: *pPointer = 84;
```

Now the memory originally pointed to by pPointer is deleted—and thus freed—in line 3.

When You Call new Don't Forget delete   For every time in your program you call new, there should be a call to delete. It is important to keep track of which pointer owns an area of memory, and to ensure that the memory is returned to the free store when you are done with it.

In this lesson you learned what a pointer is and how to use it.

LESSON 13

MORE ABOUT POINTERS

In this lesson, you will learn how to use pointers effectively and how to prevent memory problems.

CREATING OBJECTS ON THE FREE STORE

Just as you can create a pointer to an integer, you can create a pointer to any object. If you have declared an object of type Cat, you can declare a pointer to that class and instantiate a Cat object on the free store, just as you can make one on the stack. The syntax is the same as for integers:

```
Cat *pCat = new Cat;
```

This calls the default constructor—the constructor that takes no parameters. The constructor is called whenever an object is created on the stack or on the free store.

DELETING OBJECTS

When you call delete on a pointer to an object on the free store, that object's destructor is called before the memory is released. This gives your class a chance to clean up, just as it does for objects destroyed on the stack. Listing 13.1 illustrates creating and deleting objects on the free store.

LISTING 13.1   CREATING AND DELETING OBJECTS ON THE FREE STORE

```
1:      // Listing 13.1
2:      // Creating objects on the free store
3:
```

continues

LISTING 13.1   CONTINUED

```
4:        #include <iostream.h>
5:
6:        class SimpleCat
7:        {
8:        public:
9:                SimpleCat();
10:               ~SimpleCat();
11:       private:
12:               int itsAge;
13:       };
14:
15:       SimpleCat::SimpleCat()
16:       {
17:           cout << "Constructor called.\n";
18:           itsAge = 1;
19:       }
20:
21:       SimpleCat::~SimpleCat()
22:       {
23:           cout << "Destructor called.\n";
24:       }
25:
26:       int main()
27:       {
28:           cout << "SimpleCat Frisky...\n";
29:           SimpleCat Frisky;
30:           cout << "SimpleCat *pRags = new SimpleCat...\n";
31:           SimpleCat * pRags = new SimpleCat;
32:           cout << "delete pRags...\n";
33:           delete pRags;
34:           cout << "Exiting, watch Frisky go...\n";
35:           return 0;
36:       }
```

OUTPUT

```
SimpleCat Frisky...
Constructor called.
SimpleCat * pRags = new SimpleCat..
Constructor called.
delete pRags...
Destructor called.
Exiting, watch Frisky go...
Destructor called.
```

Lines 6–13 declare the stripped-down class SimpleCat. Line 9 declares
SimpleCat's constructor, and lines 15–19 contain its definition. Line 10
declares SimpleCat's destructor, and lines 21–24 contain its definition.

In line 29, `Frisky` is created on the stack, which causes the constructor to be called. In line 31, the `SimpleCat` pointed to by `pRags` is created on the heap; the constructor is called again. In line 33, delete is called on `pRags`, and the destructor is called. When the function ends, `Frisky` goes out of scope, and the destructor is called.

ACCESSING DATA MEMBERS

You accessed data members and functions by using the dot (.) operator for `Cat` objects created locally. To access the `Cat` object on the free store, you must dereference the pointer and call the dot operator on the object pointed to by the pointer. Therefore, to access the `GetAge` member function, write

```
(*pRags).GetAge();
```

Parentheses are used to assure that `pRags` is dereferenced before `GetAge()` is accessed.

Because this is cumbersome, C++ provides a shorthand operator for indirect access: the `points-to` (points-to operator)>operator (`->`), which is created by typing the dash (-) immediately followed by the greater-than symbol (>). C++ treats this as a single symbol.

MEMBER DATA ON THE FREE STORE

One or more of the data members of a class can be a pointer to an object on the free store. The memory can be allocated in the class constructor or in one of its methods, and it can be deleted in its destructor, as Listing 13.2 illustrates.

LISTING 13.2 POINTERS AS MEMBER DATA

```
1:    // Listing 13.2
2:    // Pointers as data members
3:
4:    #include <iostream.h>
5:
6:    class SimpleCat
7:    {
8:    public:
9:        SimpleCat();
```

continues

LISTING 13.2   CONTINUED

```
10:        ~SimpleCat();
11:        int GetAge() const { return *itsAge; }
12:        void SetAge(int age) { *itsAge = age; }
13:
14:        int GetWeight() const { return *itsWeight; }
15:        void setWeight (int weight){ *itsWeight = weight; }
16:
17:    private:
18:        int * itsAge;
19:        int * itsWeight;
20:    };
21:
22:    SimpleCat::SimpleCat()
23:    {
24:        itsAge = new int(2);
25:        itsWeight = new int(5);
26:    }
27:
28:    SimpleCat::~SimpleCat()
29:    {
30:        delete itsAge;
31:        delete itsWeight;
32:    }
33:
34:    int main()
35:    {
36:        SimpleCat *pFrisky = new SimpleCat;
37:        cout << "pFrisky is " << pFrisky->GetAge() <<
        ➥ " years old\n";
38:        pFrisky->SetAge(5);
39:        cout << "pFrisky is " << pFrisky->GetAge() <<
        ➥ " years old\n";
40:        delete pFrisky;
41:        return 0;
42:    }
```

OUTPUT

```
pFrisky is 2 years old
pFrisky is 5 years old
```

The class SimpleCat is declared to have two member variables—both of which are pointers to integers—on lines 18 and 19. The constructor, lines 22–26, initializes the pointers to memory on the free store and to the default values.

The destructor, lines 28–32, cleans up the allocated memory. Because this is the destructor, there is no point in assigning these pointers to null, because they will no longer be accessible. This is one of the safe places to break the rule that deleted pointers should be assigned to null, although following the rule doesn't hurt.

The calling function—in this case, main()—is unaware that itsAge and itsWeight are pointers to memory on the free store. main() continues to call GetAge() and SetAge(), and the details of the memory management are hidden in the implementation of the class—as they should be.

When pFrisky is deleted in line 40, its destructor is called. The destructor deletes each of its member pointers. If these, in turn, point to objects of other user-defined classes, their destructors are called as well.

THE this POINTER

Every class member function has a hidden parameter: the this pointer. this points to the individual object. Therefore, in each call to GetAge() or SetAge(), the this pointer for the object is included as a hidden parameter.

The job of the this pointer is to point to the individual object whose method has been invoked. Usually, you just call methods and set member variables. Occasionally, however, you'll need to access the object itself (perhaps to return a pointer to the current object). It's at that point that the this pointer becomes so helpful.

Normally, you don't need to use the this pointer to access the member variables of an object from within methods of that object. You can explicitly call the this pointer if you want to, however, this is done in Listing 13.3 to illustrate that the this pointer exists and works.

LISTING 13.3   USING THE this POINTER

```
1:     // Listing 13.3
2:     // Using the this pointer
3:
4:     #include <iostream.h>
5:
6:     class Rectangle
7:     {
```

continues

LISTING 13.3   CONTINUED

```
8:    public:
9:        Rectangle();
10:       ~Rectangle();
11:       void SetLength(int length){ this->itsLength = length;}
12:       int GetLength() const { return this->itsLength; }
13:
14:       void SetWidth(int width) { itsWidth = width; }
15:       int GetWidth() const { return itsWidth; }
16:
17:   private:
18:       int itsLength;
19:       int itsWidth;
20:   };
21:
22:   Rectangle::Rectangle()
23:   {
24:       itsWidth = 5;
25:       itsLength = 10;
26:   }
27:   Rectangle::~Rectangle()
28:   {}
29:
30:   int main()
31:   {
32:      Rectangle theRect;
33:      cout << "theRect is " << theRect.GetLength();
34:         cout << " feet long.\n";
35:      cout << "theRect is ";
36:         cout << theRect.GetWidth() << " feet wide.\n";
37:         theRect.SetLength(20);
38:         theRect.SetWidth(10);
39:         cout << "theRect is " << theRect.GetLength();
40:            cout << " feet long.\n";
41:         cout << "theRect is ";
42:            cout << theRect.GetWidth() << " feet wide.\n";
44:      return 0;
45:   }
```

```
theRect is 10 feet long
theRect is 5 feet long
theRect is 20 feet long
theRect is 10 feet long
```

The SetLength() and GetLength() accessor functions explicitly use the
this pointer to access the member variables of the Rectangle object. The
SetWidth and GetWidth accessors do not. There is no difference in their
behavior, although the versions which do not use the this pointer are easier to understand.

WHAT'S THE this POINTER FOR?

If that's all there were to the this pointer, there would be little point in
bothering you with it. The this pointer, however, is a pointer, which
means it stores the memory address of an object. As such, it can be a
powerful tool.

You'll see a practical use for the this pointer later in the book, when
operator overloading is discussed. For now, your goal is to know about the
this pointer and to understand what it is: a pointer to the object itself.

You don't have to worry about creating or deleting the this pointer. The
compiler takes care of that.

STRAY OR DANGLING POINTERS

One source of bugs that are nasty and difficult to find is stray pointers. A
stray pointer is created when you call delete on a pointer—thereby freeing the memory that it points to—and later try to use that pointer again
without reassigning it. The pointer still points to the old area of memory,
but the compiler is free to put other data there; using the pointer can cause
your program to crash. Worse, your program might proceed merrily on its
way and crash several minutes later. This is called a time bomb, and it's
no fun. To be safe, after you delete a pointer, set it to null (0). This dis-
arms the pointer.

const POINTERS

You can use the keyword const for pointers before the type, after the
type, or in both places. For example, all the following are legal declarations:

```
const int * pOne;
int * const pTwo;
const int * const pThree;
```

pOne is a pointer to a constant integer. The value that is pointed to can't be changed using this pointer. That means you can't write

```
*pOne = 5
```

If you try to do so, the compiler will object with an error.

pTwo is a constant pointer to an integer. The integer can be changed, but pTwo can't point to anything else. A constant pointer can't be reassigned. That means you can't write

```
pTwo = &x
```

pThree is a constant pointer to a constant integer. The value that is pointed to can't be changed, and pThree can't be changed to point to anything else.

Draw an imaginary line just to the right of the asterisk. If the word const is to the left of the line, that means the object is constant. If the word const is to the right of the line, the pointer itself is constant.

```
const int * p1;  // p1 can't be used to change the value of
the int to which it points
int * const p2;  // p2 can not be set to point to anything
else
```

If you declare a pointer to a const object, the only methods that you can call with that pointer are const methods.

const this POINTERS

When you declare an object to be const, you are in effect declaring that the this pointer is a pointer to a const object. A const this pointer can be used only with const member functions.

Constant objects and constant pointers will be discussed again in the next hour, when references to constant objects are discussed.

In this lesson, you learned how to access data members and methods using pointers, and you learned about the this pointer.

LESSON 14

REFERENCES

In this lesson, you will learn what references are, how references differ from pointers, how to create references and use them, what the limitations of references are, and how to pass values and objects into and out of functions by reference.

WHAT IS A REFERENCE?

References give you almost all the power of pointers but with a much easier syntax. A *reference* is an alias. When you create a reference, you initialize it with the name of another object, the target. From that moment on, the reference acts as an alternative name for the target, and anything you do to the reference is really done to the target.

That's it. Some C++ programmers will tell you that references are pointers; that is not correct. Although references are often implemented using pointers, that is a matter of concern only to creators of compilers; as a programmer you must keep these two ideas distinct.

Pointers are variables that hold the address of another object. References are aliases to another reference.

CREATING A REFERENCE

You create a reference by writing the type of the target object, followed by the reference operator (&), followed by the name of the reference. References can use any legal variable name; but for this book, prefix all reference names with r. So, if you have an integer variable named someInt, you can make a reference to that variable by writing the following:

```
int &rSomeRef = someInt;
```

This is read as "rSomeRef is a reference to integer that is initialized to refer to someInt."

Even experienced C++ programmers, who know the rule that references cannot be reassigned and are always aliases for their target, can be confused by what happens when you try to reassign a reference. What appears to be a reassignment turns out to be the assignment of a new value to the target. Listing 14.1 illustrates this fact.

LISTING **14.1** ASSIGNING TO A REFERENCE

```
1:      //Listing 14.1
2:      //Reassigning a reference
3:
4:      #include <iostream.h>
5:
6:      int main()
7:      {
8:          int   intOne;
9:          int &rSomeRef = intOne;
10:
11:         intOne = 5;
12:         cout << "intOne:\t" << intOne << endl;
13:         cout << "rSomeRef:\t" << rSomeRef << endl;
14:         cout << "&intOne:\t" << &intOne << endl;
15:         cout << "&rSomeRef:\t" << &rSomeRef << endl;
16:
17:         int intTwo = 8;
18:         rSomeRef = intTwo;  // not what you think!
19:         cout << "\nintOne:\t" << intOne << endl;
20:         cout << "intTwo:\t" << intTwo << endl;
21:         cout << "rSomeRef:\t" << rSomeRef << endl;
22:         cout << "&intOne:\t" << &intOne << endl;
23:         cout << "&intTwo:\t" << &intTwo << endl;
24:         cout << "&rSomeRef:\t" << &rSomeRef << endl;
25:         return 0;
26:     }
```

OUTPUT

```
intOne:      5
rSomeRef:    5
&intOne:     0x0012FF7C
&rSomeRef:   0x0012FF7C

intOne:      8
intTwo:      8
rSomeRef:    8
```

```
&intOne:      0x0012FF7C
&intTwo:      0x0012FF74
&rSomeRef:    0x0012FF7C
```

An integer variable and a reference to an integer are declared, on lines 8 and 9. The integer is assigned the value 5 on line 11, and the values and their addresses are printed on lines 12–15.

On line 17, a new variable, intTwo, is created and initialized with the value 8. On line 18 the programmer tries to reassign rSomeRef to now be an alias to the variable intTwo, but that is not what happens. What actually happens is that rSomeRef continues to act as an alias for intOne, so this assignment is exactly equivalent to the following:

```
intOne = intTwo;
```

Sure enough, when the values of intOne and rSomeRef are printed (lines 19–21) they are the same as intTwo. In fact, when the addresses are printed on lines 22–24, you see that rSomeRef continues to refer to intOne and not intTwo.

WHAT CAN BE REFERENCED?

Any object can be referenced, including user-defined objects.

References to objects are used just like the object itself. Member data and methods are accessed using the normal class member access operator (.), and just as with the built-in types, the reference acts as an alias to the object.

NULL POINTERS AND NULL REFERENCES

When pointers are not initialized, or when they are deleted, they ought to be assigned to null (0). This is not true for references. In fact, a reference cannot be null, and a program with a reference to a null object is considered an invalid program. When a program is invalid, just about anything can happen. It can appear to work, or it can erase all the files on your disk. Both are possible outcomes of an invalid program.

Most compilers will support a null object without much complaint, crashing only if you try to use the object in some way. Taking advantage of this, however, is still not a good idea. When you move your program to another machine or compiler, mysterious bugs might develop if you have null objects.

PASSING FUNCTION ARGUMENTS BY REFERENCE

In Lesson 6, "Functions," you learned that functions have two limitations: arguments are passed by value, and the return statement can return only one value.

Passing values to a function by reference can overcome both of these limitations. In C++, passing by reference is accomplished in two ways: using pointers and using references. The syntax is different, but the net effect is the same: rather than a copy being created within the scope of the function, the actual original object is passed into the function.

Passing an object by reference enables the function to change the object being referred to.

Listing 14.2 creates a swap function and passes in its parameters by value.

LISTING 14.2   DEMONSTRATING PASS BY VALUE

```
1:    //Listing 14.2 Demonstrates passing by value
2:
3:    #include <iostream.h>
4:
5:    void swap(int x, int y);
6:
7:    int main()
8:    {
9:        int x = 5, y = 10;
10:
11:       cout << "Main. Before swap, x: " << x <<
          ➥ " y: " << y << "\n";
12:       swap(x,y);
13:       cout << "Main. After swap, x: " << x <<
          ➥ " y: " << y << "\n";
14:       return 0;
15:   }
16:
```

```
17:   void swap (int x, int y)
18:   {
19:       int temp;
20:
21:       cout << "Swap. Before swap, x: " << x <<
      ➥ " y: " << y << "\n";
22:
23:       temp = x;
24:       x = y;
25:       y = temp;
26:
27:       cout << "Swap. After swap, x: " << x <<
      ➥ " y: " << y << "\n";
28:
29:   }
```

```
Main. Before swap. x: 5 y: 10
Swap. Before swap. x: 5 y: 10
Swap. After swap. x: 10 y: 5
Main. After swap. x: 5 y: 10
```
OUTPUT

This program initializes two variables in main() and then passes them to the swap() function, which appears to swap them. But when they are examined again in main(), they are unchanged!

The problem here is that x and y are being passed to swap() by value. That is, local copies were made in the function. What you want is to pass x and y by reference.

There are two ways to solve this problem in C++: you can make the parameters of swap() pointers to the original values, or you can pass in references to the original values.

MAKING swap() WORK WITH POINTERS

When you pass in a pointer, you pass in the address of the object, and thus the function can manipulate the value at that address. To make swap() change the actual values using pointers, the function, swap(), should be declared to accept two int pointers. Then, by dereferencing the pointers, the values of x and y will, in fact, be swapped. Listing 14.3 demonstrates this idea.

LISTING 14.3   PASSING BY REFERENCE USING POINTERS

```
1:     //Listing 14.3 Demonstrates passing by reference
2:
3:     #include <iostream.h>
4:
5:     void swap(int *x, int *y);
6:
7:     int main()
8:     {
9:         int x = 5, y = 10;
10:
11:        cout << "Main. Before swap, x: " << x <<
       ➥ " y: " << y << "\n";
12        swap(&x,&y);
13:        cout << "Main. After swap, x: " << x <<
       ➥ " y: " << y << "\n";
14:        return 0;
15:    }
16
17:    void swap (int *px, int *py)
18:    {
19:        int temp;
20:
21:        cout << "Swap. Before swap, *px: ";
22:        cout << *px << " *py: " << *py << "\n";
23:
24:        temp = *px;
25:        *px = *py;
26:        *py = temp;
27:
28:        cout << "Swap. After swap, *px: ";
29:        cout << *px << " *py: " << *py << "\n";
30:
31:    }
```

OUTPUT

```
Main. Before swap. x: 5 y: 10
Swap. Before swap. *px: 5 *py: 10
Swap. After swap. *px: 10 *py: 5
Main. After swap. x: 10 y: 5
```

Success! On line 5, the prototype of swap() is changed to indicate that its two parameters will be pointers to int rather than int variables. When swap() is called on line 12, the addresses of x and y are passed as the arguments.

On line 19, a local variable, temp, is declared in the swap() function. Temp need not be a pointer; it will just hold the value of *px (that is, the value of x in the calling function) for the life of the function. After the function returns, temp will no longer be needed.

On line 23, temp is assigned the value at px. On line 24, the value at px is assigned to the value at py. On line 25, the value stashed in temp (that is, the original value at px) is put into py.

The net effect of this is that the values in the calling function, whose address was passed to swap(), are in fact swapped.

IMPLEMENTING swap() WITH REFERENCES

The preceding program works, but the syntax of the swap() function is cumbersome in two ways. First, the repeated need to dereference the pointers within the swap() function makes it error-prone and hard to read. Second, the need to pass the address of the variables in the calling function makes the inner workings of swap() overly apparent to its users.

It is a goal of C++ to prevent the user of a function from worrying about how it works. Passing by pointers puts the burden on the calling function, where it belongs, rather than on the called function. Listing 14.4 rewrites the swap() function using references.

LISTING 14.4   swap() REWRITTEN WITH REFERENCES

```
1:   /Listing 14.4 Demonstrates passing by reference
2:   / using references!
3:
4:   #include <iostream.h>
5:
6:   void swap(int &x, int &y);
7:
8:   int main()
9:   {
10:       int x = 5, y = 10;
11:
12:       cout << "Main. Before swap, x: "<< x <<
          ➥" y: " << y << "\n";
13:       swap(x,y);
14:       cout << "Main. After swap, x: "<< x <<
          ➥" y: " << y << "\n";
15:       return 0;
16:   }
```

continues

LISTING 14.4   Continued

```
17:
18: void swap (int &rx, int &ry)
19: {
20:         int temp;
21:         cout << "Swap. Before swap, rx: ";
22:         cout << rx << " ry: " << ry << "\n";
23:
24:         temp = rx;
25:         rx = ry;
26:         ry = temp;
27:         cout << "Swap. After swap, rx: ";
28:         cout << rx << " ry: " << ry << "\n";
29:
30:       }
```

```
Main. Before swap, x:5 y: 10
Swap. Before swap, rx:5 ry:10
Swap. After swap, rx:10 ry:5
Main. After swap, x:10, y:5
```

Just as in the example with pointers, two variables are declared on line 10, and their values are printed on line 12. On line 13 the function swap() is called, but note that x and y are passed, not their addresses. The calling function simply passes the variables.

When swap() is called, program execution jumps to line 18, where the variables are identified as references. Their values are printed on lines 21 and 22, but note that no special operators are required. These are aliases for the original values, and can be used as such.

On lines 24–26 the values are swapped, and then they're printed on lines 27 and 28. Program execution jumps back to the calling function, and on line 14 the values are printed in main(). Because the parameters to swap() are declared to be references, the values from main() are passed by reference and thus are changed in main() as well.

References provide the convenience and ease of use of normal variables, with the power and pass-by-reference capability of pointers!

RETURNING MULTIPLE VALUES

As discussed, functions can only return one value. What if you need to get two values back from a function? One way to solve this problem is to pass two objects into the function, by reference. The function can then fill the objects with the correct values. Because passing by reference enables a function to change the original objects, this effectively lets the function return two pieces of information. This approach bypasses the return value of the function, which can then be reserved for reporting errors.

Once again, this can be done with references or pointers. Listing 14.5 demonstrates a function that returns three values, two as pointer parameters and one as the return value of the function.

LISTING 14.5   RETURNING VALUES WITH POINTERS

```
1:     //Listing 14.5
2:     // Returning multiple values from a function
3:
4:     #include <iostream.h>
5:
6:
7:
8:     short Factor(int, int*, int*);
9:
10:    int main()
11:    {
12:        int number, squared, cubed;
13:        short error;
14:
15:        cout << "Enter a number (0 - 20): ";
16:        cin >> number;
17:
18:        error = Factor(number, &squared, &cubed);
19:
20:        if (!error)
21:        {
22:            cout << "number: " << number << "\n";
23:            cout << "square: " << squared << "\n";
24:            cout << "cubed: "  << cubed   << "\n";
25:        }
26:        else
27:            cout << "Error encountered!!\n";
28:        return 0;
29:    }
30:
```

continues

LISTING **14.5**   CONTINUED

```
31:    short Factor(int n, int *pSquared, int *pCubed)
32:    {
33:        short Value = 0;
34:        if (n > 20)
35:            Value = 1;
36:        else
37:        {
38:            *pSquared = n*n;
39:            *pCubed = n*n*n;
40:            Value = 0;
41:        }
42:        return Value;
43:    }
```

OUTPUT

```
Enter a number (0-20): 3
number: 3
square: 9
cubed: 27
```

On line 12, number, squared, and cubed are defined as ints. number is assigned a value based on user input. This number and the addresses of squared and cubed are passed to the function Factor().

Factor() examines the first parameter, which is passed by value. If it is greater than 20 (the maximum value this function can handle), it sets return Value to a simple error value. Note that the return value from Function() is reserved for either this error value or the value 0, indicating all went well; also note that the function returns this value on line 42.

The actual values needed, the square and cube of number, are returned not by using the return mechanism, but rather by changing the pointers that were passed into the function.

On lines 38 and 39, the pointers are assigned their return values. On line 40, return Value is assigned a success value. On line 42, return Value is returned.

One improvement to this program might be to declare the following:

```
enum ERROR_VALUE { SUCCESS, FAILURE};
```

Then, rather than returning 0 or 1, the program could return SUCCESS or FAILURE.

RETURNING VALUES BY REFERENCE

Although Listing 14.5 works, it can be made easier to read and maintain by using references rather than pointers. Listing 14.6 shows the same program rewritten to use references and to incorporate the ERROR enumeration.

LISTING **14.6**   LISTING **14.5** REWRITTEN USING REFERENCES

```
1:      //Listing 14.6
2:      // Returning multiple values from a function
3:      // using references
4:
5:      #include <iostream.h>
6:
7:
8:      enum ERR_CODE { SUCCESS, ERROR };
9:
10:     ERR_CODE Factor(int, int&, int&);
11:
12:     int main()
13:     {
14:            int number, squared, cubed;
15:            ERR_CODE result;
16:
17:            cout << "Enter a number (0 - 20): ";
18:            cin >> number;
19:
20:            result = Factor(number, squared, cubed);
21:
22:            if (result == SUCCESS)
23:            {
24:                cout << "number: " << number << "\n";
25:                cout << "square: " << squared << "\n";
26:                cout << "cubed: "  << cubed   << "\n";
27:            }
28:            else
29:                cout << "Error encountered!!\n";
30:            return 0;
31:     }
32:
33:     ERR_CODE Factor(int n, int &rSquared, int &rCubed)
34:     {
35:            if (n > 20)
36:                return ERROR;    //simple error code
```

continues

LISTING 14.6   CONTINUED

```
37:             else
38:             {
39:                     rSquared = n*n;
40:                     rCubed = n*n*n;
41:                     return SUCCESS;
42:             }
43:     }
```

```
Enter a number

 (0-20): 3
number: 3
square: 9
cubed: 27
```

Listing 14.6 is identical to 14.5, with two exceptions. The ERR_CODE enumeration makes the error reporting a bit more explicit on lines 36 and 41, as well as the error handling on line 22.

The larger change, however, is that Factor() is now declared to take references to squared and cubed rather than to pointers. This makes the manipulation of these parameters far simpler and easier to understand.

In this lesson, you learned how to use references and how to pass by reference using references or pointers.

LESSON 15

ADVANCED REFERENCES AND POINTERS

In this lesson, you will learn how to use pass by reference, how to decide when to use references and when to use pointers, how to avoid memory problems when using pointers, and how to avoid the pitfalls of using references.

PASSING BY REFERENCE FOR EFFICIENCY

Each time you pass an object into a function by value, a copy of the object is made. Each time you return an object from a function by value, another copy is made.

With larger, user-created objects, the cost of these copies is substantial. You'll use more memory than you need to, and ultimately your program will run slower.

The size of a user-created object on the stack is the sum of each of its member variables. These, in turn, can each be user-created objects, and passing such a massive structure by copying it onto the stack can be very expensive in terms of performance and memory consumption.

There is another cost as well. With the classes you create, each of these temporary copies is created when the compiler calls a special constructor: the copy constructor. In Lesson 16 "Advanced Funtions," you will learn how copy constructors work and how you can make your own, but for now it is enough to know that the copy constructor is called each time a temporary copy of the object is put on the stack.

When the temporary object is destroyed, which happens when the function returns, the object's destructor is called. If an object is returned by value, a copy of that object must be made and destroyed as well.

With large objects, these constructor and destructor calls can be expensive in speed and use of memory. To illustrate this idea, Listing 15.1 creates a stripped-down, user-created object: SimpleCat. A real object would be larger and more expensive, but this is sufficient to show how often the copy constructor and destructor are called.

Listing 15.1 creates the SimpleCat object and then calls two functions. The first function receives the Cat by value and then returns it by value. The second one receives a pointer to the object, rather than the object itself, and returns a pointer to the object.

Listing 15.1 PASSING OBJECTS BY REFERENCE

```
1:    //Listing 15.1
2:    // Passing pointers to objects
3:
4:    #include <iostream.h>
5:
6:    class SimpleCat
7:    {
8:    public:
9:             SimpleCat ();              // constructor
10:            SimpleCat(SimpleCat&);     // copy constructor
11:            ~SimpleCat();              // destructor
12:    };
13:
14:    SimpleCat::SimpleCat()
15:    {
16:            cout << "Simple Cat Constructor...\n";
17:    }
18:
19:    SimpleCat::SimpleCat(SimpleCat& rhs)
20:    {
21:            cout << "Simple Cat Copy Constructor...\n";
22:    }
23:
24:    SimpleCat::~SimpleCat()
25:    {
26:            cout << "Simple Cat Destructor...\n";
27:    }
28:
```

```
29:    SimpleCat FunctionOne (SimpleCat theCat);
30:    SimpleCat* FunctionTwo (SimpleCat *theCat);
31:
32:    int main()
33:    {
34:            cout << "Making a cat...\n";
35:            SimpleCat Frisky;
36:            cout << "Calling FunctionOne...\n";
37:            FunctionOne(Frisky);
38:            cout << "Calling FunctionTwo...\n";
39:            FunctionTwo(&Frisky);
40:            return 0;
41:    }
42:
43:    // FunctionOne, passes by value
44:    SimpleCat FunctionOne(SimpleCat theCat)
45:    {
46:            cout << "Function One. Returning...\n";
47:            return theCat;
48:    }
49:
50:    // functionTwo, passes by reference
51:    SimpleCat* FunctionTwo (SimpleCat   *theCat)
52:    {
53:            cout << "Function Two. Returning...\n";
54:            return theCat;
55:    }
```

```
1:  Making a cat...
2:  Simple Cat Constructor...
3:  Calling FunctionOne...
4:  Simple Cat Copy Constructor...
5:  Function One. Returning...
6:  Simple Cat Copy Constructor...
7:  Simple Cat Destructor...
8:  Simple Cat Destructor...
9:  Calling FunctionTwo...
10: Function Two. Returning...
11: Simple Cat Destructor...
```

OUTPUT

Line Numbers in the Output   The line numbers shown here will not print. They were added to aid in the analysis.

A very simplified SimpleCat class is declared on lines 6–12. The constructor, copy constructor, and destructor all print an informative message so you can tell when they've been called.

On line 34, main() prints out a message; you can see it on output line 1. On line 35, a SimpleCat object is instantiated. This causes the constructor to be called, and the output from the constructor is shown on output line 2.

On line 36, main() reports that it is calling FunctionOne(), which creates output line 3. Because FunctionOne() is called passing the SimpleCat object by value, a copy of the SimpleCat object is made on the stack as an object local to the called function. This causes the copy constructor to be called, which creates output line 4.

Program execution jumps to line 45 in the called function, which prints an informative message, output line 5. The function then returns, returning the SimpleCat object by value. This creates yet another copy of the object, calling the copy constructor and producing line 6.

The return value from FunctionOne() is not assigned to any object, so the temporary object created for the return is thrown away, calling the destructor, which produces output line 7. Because FunctionOne() has ended, its local copy goes out of scope and is destroyed, calling the destructor and producing line 8.

Program execution returns to main(), and FunctionTwo() is called, but the parameter is passed by reference. No copy is produced, so there's no output. FunctionTwo() prints the message that appears as output line 10 and then returns the SimpleCat object, again by reference, and so again produces no calls to the constructor or destructor.

Finally, the program ends and Frisky goes out of scope, causing one final call to the destructor and printing output line 11.

The net effect of this is that the call to FunctionOne(), because it passed the cat by value, produced two calls to the copy constructor and two to the destructor, although the call to FunctionTwo() produced none.

PASSING A const POINTER

Although passing a pointer to FunctionTwo() is more efficient, it is dangerous. FunctionTwo() is not allowed to change the SimpleCat object it is passed, yet it is given the address of the SimpleCat. This seriously exposes the object to change and defeats the protection offered in passing by value.

Passing by value is like giving a museum a photograph of your masterpiece instead of the real thing. If vandals mark it up, there is no harm done to the original. Passing by reference is like sending your home address to the museum and inviting guests to come over and look at the real thing.

The solution is to pass a const pointer to SimpleCat. Doing so prevents calling any non-const method on SimpleCat, and thus protects the object from change.

REFERENCES AS AN ALTERNATIVE

Using constant pointers is cumbersome, and references present an attractive alternative. Listing 15.2 illustrates.

Listing 15.2   PASSING REFERENCES TO OBJECTS

```
1:     //Listing 15.2
2:     // Passing references to objects
3:
4:     #include <iostream.h>
5:
6:     class SimpleCat
7:     {
8:     public:
9:             SimpleCat();
10:            SimpleCat(SimpleCat&);
11:            ~SimpleCat();
12:
13:            int GetAge() const { return itsAge; }
14:            void SetAge(int age) { itsAge = age; }
15:
16:    private:
17:            int itsAge;
18:    };
19:
20:    SimpleCat::SimpleCat()
21:    {
22:            cout << "Simple Cat Constructor...\n";
```

continues

Listing 15.2   CONTINUED

```
23:              itsAge = 1;
24:  }
25:
26:  SimpleCat::SimpleCat(SimpleCat&)
27:  {
28:          cout << "Simple Cat Copy Constructor...\n";
29:  }
30:
31:  SimpleCat::~SimpleCat()
32:  {
33:          cout << "Simple Cat Destructor...\n";
34:  }
35:
36:  const      SimpleCat & FunctionTwo
     ➡(const SimpleCat & theCat);
37:
38:  int main()
39:  {
40:          cout << "Making a cat...\n";
41:          SimpleCat Frisky;
42:          cout << "Frisky is " << Frisky.GetAge()
             ➡<< " years old\n";
43:          int age = 5;
44:          Frisky.SetAge(age);
45:          cout << "Frisky is " << Frisky.GetAge()
             ➡<< " years old\n";
46:          cout << "Calling FunctionTwo...\n";
47:          FunctionTwo(Frisky);
48:          cout << "Frisky is " << Frisky.GetAge()
             ➡<< " years old\n";
49:          return 0;
50:  }
51:
52:  // functionTwo passes a ref to a const object
53:  const SimpleCat & FunctionTwo (const SimpleCat & theCat)
54:  {
55:          cout << "Function Two. Returning...\n";
56:          cout << "Frisky is now " << theCat.GetAge();
57:          cout << " years old \n";
58:          // theCat.SetAge(8);    const!
59:          return theCat;
60:  }
```

```
Making a cat...
Simple Cat constructor...
Frisky is 1 years old
Frisky is 5 years old
Calling FunctionTwo
FunctionTwo. Returning...
Frisky is now 5 years old
Frisky is 5 years old
Simple Cat Destructor...
```

WHEN TO USE REFERENCES AND WHEN TO USE POINTERS

C++ programmers strongly prefer references to pointers. References are cleaner and easier to use, and they do a better job of hiding information, as you saw in the previous example.

References cannot be reassigned. If you need to point first to one object and then to another, you must use a pointer. References cannot be null, so if there is any chance that the object in question might be null, you must not use a reference. You must use a pointer.

DON'T RETURN A REFERENCE TO AN OBJECT THAT ISN'T IN SCOPE!

After C++ programmers learn to pass by reference, they have a tendency to go hog-wild. It is possible, however, to overdo it. Remember that a reference is always an alias to some other object. If you pass a reference into or out of a function, be sure to ask yourself, "What is the object I'm aliasing, and will it still exist every time it's used?"

Listing 15.3 illustrates the danger of returning a reference to an object that no longer exists.

LISTING 15.3   RETURNING A REFERENCE TO A NONEXISTENT OBJECT

```
1:      // Listing 15.3
2:      // Returning a reference to an object
3:      // which no longer exists
4:
5:      #include <iostream.h>
6:
7:      class SimpleCat
8:      {
9:      public:
10:             SimpleCat (int age, int weight);
11:             ~SimpleCat() {}
12:             int GetAge() const { return itsAge; }
13:             int GetWeight() const { return itsWeight; }
14:      private:
15:             int itsAge;
16:             int itsWeight;
17:      };
18:
19:      SimpleCat::SimpleCat(int age, int weight):
20:      itsAge(age), itsWeight(weight) {}
21:
22:      SimpleCat &TheFunction();
23:
24:      int main()
25:      {
26:             SimpleCat &rCat = TheFunction();
27:             int age = rCat.GetAge();
28:             cout << "rCat is " << age << " years old!\n";
29:             return 0;
30:      }
31:
32:      SimpleCat &TheFunction()
33:      {
34:             SimpleCat Frisky(5,9);
35:             return Frisky;
36:      }
```

Compile error: Attempting to return a
reference to a local object!

Compiler Incompatibility   This program won't compile on the Borland compiler. It will compile on Microsoft compilers; however, it should be noted that this is a bad coding practice.

On lines 7–17, SimpleCat is declared. On line 26, a reference to SimpleCat is initialized with the results of calling TheFunction(), which is declared on line 22 to return a reference to a SimpleCat.

The body of TheFunction() declares a local object of type SimpleCat and initializes its age and weight. It then returns that local object by reference. Some compilers are smart enough to catch this error and won't let you run the program. Others will let you run the program but with unpredictable results.

When TheFunction() returns, the local object, Frisky, will be destroyed (painlessly, I assure you). The reference returned by this function will be an alias to a nonexistent object, and this is a bad thing.

RETURNING A REFERENCE TO AN OBJECT ON THE HEAP

You might be tempted to solve the problem in Listing 15.3 by having TheFunction() create Frisky on the heap. That way, when you return from TheFunction(), Frisky will still exist.

The problem with this approach is: What do you do with the memory allocated for Frisky when you are done with it? Listing 15.4 illustrates this problem.

Listing 15.4 MEMORY LEAKS

```
1:       // Listing 15.4
2:       // Resolving memory leaks
3:       #include <iostream.h>
4:
5:       class SimpleCat
6:       {
7:       public:
8:               SimpleCat (int age, int weight);
9:               ~SimpleCat() {}
10:              int GetAge() const { return itsAge; }
11:              int GetWeight() const { return itsWeight; }
12:
13       private:
14:              int itsAge;
```

continues

Listing 15.4 CONTINUED

```
15:             int itsWeight;
16:     };
17:
18:     SimpleCat::SimpleCat(int age, int weight):
19:     itsAge(age), itsWeight(weight) {}
20:
21:     SimpleCat & TheFunction();
22:
23:     int main()
24:     {
25:             SimpleCat & rCat = TheFunction();
26:             int age = rCat.GetAge();
27:             cout << "rCat is " << age << " years old!\n";
28:             cout << "&rCat: " << &rCat << endl;
29:             // How do you get rid of that memory?
30:             SimpleCat * pCat = &rCat;
31:             delete pCat;
32:             // Uh oh, rCat now refers to ??
33:             return 0;
34:     }
35:
36:     SimpleCat &TheFunction()
37:     {
38:             SimpleCat * pFrisky = new SimpleCat(5,9);
39:             cout << "pFrisky: " << pFrisky << endl;
40:             return *pFrisky;
41:     }
```

OUTPUT

```
pFrisky: 0x00431CA0
rCat is 5 years old!
&rCat: 0x00431CA0
```

> **A Working but Flawed Program**   This compiles, links, and appears to work. But it is a time bomb waiting to go off.

The function TheFunction() has been changed so that it no longer returns a reference to a local variable. Memory is allocated on the free store and assigned to a pointer on line 38. The address that pointer holds is printed, and then the pointer is dereferenced and the SimpleCat object is returned by reference.

On line 25, the return of `TheFunction()` is assigned to a reference to a `SimpleCat`, and that object is used to obtain the cat's age, which is printed on line 27.

To prove that the reference declared in `main()` is referring to the object put on the free store in `TheFunction()`, the address of operator is applied to `rCat`. Sure enough, it displays the address of the object it refers to, and this matches the address of the object on the free store.

So far, so good, but how will that memory be freed? You can't call `delete` on the reference. One clever solution is to create another pointer and initialize it with the address obtained from `rCat`. This does delete the memory and plugs the memory leak. One small problem though: What is `rCat` referring to after line 31? As stated earlier, a reference must always alias an actual object; if it references a null object (as this does now), the program is invalid.

Avoid References to Null Objects   It cannot be overemphasized that a program with a reference to a null object can compile, but it is invalid and its performance is unpredictable.

There are actually three solutions to this problem. The first is to declare a `SimpleCat` object on line 25, and to return that cat from `TheFunction()` by value. The second is to go ahead and declare the `SimpleCat` on the free store in `TheFunction()`, but have `TheFunction()` return a pointer to that memory. Then the calling function can delete the pointer when it is done.

The third workable solution, and the right one, is to declare the object in the calling function and then to pass it to `TheFunction()` by reference.

POINTER, POINTER, WHO HAS THE POINTER?

When your program allocates memory on the free store, a pointer is returned. It is imperative that you keep a pointer to that memory, because when the pointer is lost, the memory cannot be deleted and becomes a memory leak.

As you pass this block of memory between functions, someone will "own" the pointer. Typically the value in the block will be passed using references, and the function that created the memory is the one that deletes it. But this is a general rule, not an ironclad one.

It is dangerous for one function to create memory and another to free it, however. Ambiguity about who owns the pointer can lead to one of two problems: forgetting to delete a pointer or deleting it twice. Either one can cause serious problems in your program. It is safer to build your functions so that they delete the memory they create.

If you are writing a function that needs to create memory and then pass it back to the calling function, consider changing your interface. Have the calling function allocate the memory and then pass it into your function by reference. This moves all memory management out of your program and back to the function that is prepared to delete it.

In this lesson, you learned how to pass by reference, when to use pointers, and when to use references.

LESSON 16
ADVANCED FUNCTIONS

In this lesson, you will learn how to overload member functions and how to write functions to support classes with dynamically allocated variables.

OVERLOADED MEMBER FUNCTIONS

In Lesson 6, "Functions," you learned how to implement function poly-morphism, or function overloading, by writing two or more functions with the same name but with different parameters. Class member functions can also be overloaded in exactly the same way, and just as non-class func-tions can have one or more default values, so can each member function of a class.

CHOOSING BETWEEN DEFAULT VALUES AND OVERLOADED FUNCTIONS

Look to function overloading when

- There is no reasonable default value.
- You need different algorithms.
- You need to support different types in your parameter list.

THE DEFAULT CONSTRUCTOR

As discussed in Lesson 8, "More About Classes," if you do not explicitly declare a constructor for your class, a default constructor is created that takes no parameters and does nothing. You are free to make your own default constructor, however, that takes no arguments but that sets up your object as required.

The constructor provided for you is called the default constructor, but by convention, so is any constructor that takes no parameters. This can be a bit confusing, but it is usually clear from context.

Take note that if you make any constructors at all, the default constructor is not made by the compiler. So if you want a constructor that takes no parameters, and you've created any other constructors, you must make the default constructor yourself!

Overloading Constructors

A constructor is used to create an object.

Constructors, like all member functions, can be overloaded. The capability to overload constructors is very powerful and very flexible.

For example, you might have a rectangle object that has two constructors. The first takes a length and a width and makes a rectangle of that size. The second takes no values and makes a default-sized rectangle. The compiler chooses the right constructor just as it does any overloaded function: based on the number and type of the parameters.

Whereas you can overload constructors, you cannot overload destructors. Destructors, by definition, always have exactly the same signature: the name of the class prepended by a tilde (~) and no parameters.

Initializing Objects

Up until now, you've been setting the member variables of objects in the body of the constructor. Constructors, however, are created in two stages: the initialization stage and then the body of the constructor.

Most variables can be set in either stage, either by initializing in the initialization stage or by assigning in the body of the constructor. It is cleaner, and often more efficient, to initialize member variables at the initialization stage. The following example shows how to initialize member variables:

```
CAT():          // constructor name and parameters
itsAge(5),      // initialization list
itsWeight(8)
{ }             // body of constructor
```

After the closing parentheses on the constructor's parameter list, put a colon. Then put the name of the member variable and a pair of parentheses. Inside the parentheses, put the expression to be used to initialize that member variable. If there is more than one initialization, separate each one with a comma.

Remember that references and constants must be initialized and cannot be assigned to. If you have references or constants as member data, these must be initialized as shown here.

Earlier, I said it is more efficient to initialize member variables rather than to assign to them. To understand this, you must first understand the copy constructor.

THE COPY CONSTRUCTOR

In addition to providing a default constructor and destructor, the compiler provides a default copy constructor. The copy constructor is called every time a copy of an object is made.

When you pass an object by value, either into a function or as a function's return value, a temporary copy of that object is made. If the object is a user-defined object, the class's copy constructor is called.

All copy constructors take one parameter: a reference to an object of the same class. It is a good idea to make it a constant reference, because the constructor will not have to alter the object passed in. For example:

```
CAT(const CAT & theCat);
```

Here the CAT constructor takes a constant reference to an existing CAT object. The goal of the copy constructor is to make a copy of theCat.

The default copy constructor simply copies each member variable from the object passed as a parameter to the member variables of the new object. This is called a *member-wise* (or *shallow*) copy, and although this is fine for most member variables, it breaks pretty quickly for member variables that are pointers to objects on the free store.

Shallow and Deep Copies   A shallow or member-wise copy copies the exact values of one object's member valuables into another object. Pointers in both objects end up pointing to the same memory. A deep copy, on the other hand, copies the values allocated on the heap to newly allocated memory.

If the CAT class includes a member variable, itsAge, that points to an integer on the free store, the default copy constructor will copy the passed-in CAT's itsAge member variable to the new CAT's itsAge member variable. The two objects will then point to the same memory, as illustrated in Figure 16.1.

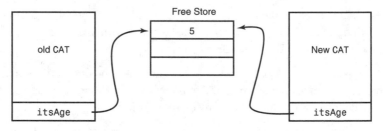

FIGURE **16.1**   Using the default copy constructor.

This will lead to a disaster when either CAT goes out of scope. When the object goes out of scope, the destructor is called, and it will attempt to clean up the allocated memory.

In this case, let's say the original CAT goes out of scope. Its destructor will free the allocated memory. The copy will still be pointing to that memory, however, and if it tries to access that memory it will crash your program, if you're lucky. Figure 16.2 illustrates this problem.

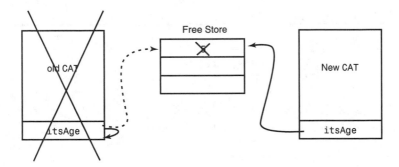

FIGURE **16.2**   Creating a stray pointer.

The solution to this is to define your own copy constructor and to allocate memory as required in the copy. After the memory is allocated, the old values can be copied into the new memory. This is called a *deep copy*. Listing 16.1 illustrates how to do this.

LISTING **16.1**   COPY CONSTRUCTORS

```
1:    // Listing 16.1
2:    // Copy constructors
3:
4:    #include <iostream.h>
5:
6:    class CAT
7:    {
8:    public:
9:          CAT();                    //
             ➥default constructor
10:          CAT (const CAT &);       // copy constructor
11:          ~CAT();                  // destructor
12:          int GetAge() const { return *itsAge; }
13:          int GetWeight() const
             ➥{ return *itsWeight; }
14:          void SetAge(int age) { *itsAge = age; }
15:
16:    private:
17:          int *itsAge;
18:          int *itsWeight;
19:    };
20:
21:    CAT::CAT()
```

continues

LISTING 16.1 CONTINUED

```
22:   {
23:         itsAge = new int;
24:         itsWeight = new int;
25:         *itsAge = 5;
26:         *itsWeight = 9;
27:   }
28:
29:   CAT::CAT(const CAT & rhs)
30:   {
31:         itsAge = new int;
32:         itsWeight = new int;
33:         *itsAge = rhs.GetAge();
34:         *itsWeight = rhs.GetWeight();
35:   }
36:
37:   CAT::~CAT()
38:   {
39:         delete itsAge;
40:         itsAge = 0;
41:         delete itsWeight;
42:         itsWeight = 0;
43:   }
44:
45:   int main()
46:   {
47:         CAT frisky;
48:         cout << "frisky's age: "
              ➥<< frisky.GetAge() << endl;
49:         cout << "Setting frisky to 6...\n";
50:         frisky.SetAge(6);
51:         cout << "Creating boots from frisky\n";
52:         CAT boots(frisky);
53:         cout << "frisky's age: "
              ➥<< frisky.GetAge() << endl;
54:         cout << "boots' age: "
              ➥<< boots.GetAge() << endl;
55:         cout << "setting frisky to 7...\n";
56:         frisky.SetAge(7);
57:         cout << "frisky's age: "
              ➥<< frisky.GetAge() << endl;
58:         cout << "boot's age: "
              ➥<< boots.GetAge() << endl;
59:         return 0;
60:   }
```

```
frisky's age: 5
Setting frisky to 6...
Creating boots from frisky
frisky's age: 6
boots' age:  6
setting frisky to 7...
frisky's age: 7
boots' age: 6
```

On lines 6–19, the CAT class is declared. Note that on line 9 a default constructor is declared, and on line 10 a copy constructor is declared.

On lines 17 and 18, two member variables are declared, each as a pointer to an integer. Typically there'd be little reason for a class to store int member variables as pointers, but this was done to illustrate how to manage member variables on the free store.

The default constructor, on lines 21–27, allocates room on the free store for two int variables and then assigns values to them.

The copy constructor begins on line 29. Note that the parameter is rhs. It is common to refer to the parameter to a copy constructor as rhs, which stands for right-hand side. When you look at the assignments in lines 33 and 34, you'll see that the object passed in as a parameter is on the right-hand side of the equal sign. Here's how it works:

- On lines 31 and 32, memory is allocated on the free store. Then, on lines 33 and 34, the value at the new memory location is assigned the values from the existing CAT.

- The parameter rhs is a CAT that is passed into the copy constructor as a constant reference. The member function rhs.GetAge() returns the value stored in the memory pointed to by rhs's member variable itsAge. As a CAT object, rhs has all the member variables of any other CAT.

- When the copy constructor is called to create a new CAT, an existing CAT is passed in as a parameter.

Figure 16.2 diagrams what is happening here. The values pointed to by the existing CAT are copied to the memory allocated for the new CAT.

On line 47, a CAT is created, called frisky. frisky's age is printed, and then his age is set to 6 on line 50. On line 52, a new CAT is created, boots, using the copy constructor, and passing in frisky. Had frisky been passed as a parameter to a function, this same call to the copy constructor would have been made by the compiler.

On lines 53 and 54, the ages of both CATs are printed. Sure enough, boots has frisky's age, 6, not the default age of 5. On line 56, frisky's age is set to 7, and then the ages are printed again. This time, frisky's age is 7, but boots' age is still 6, demonstrating that they are stored in separate areas of memory.

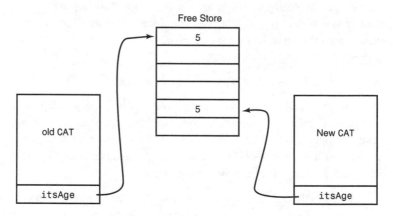

FIGURE 16.3   An illustration of a deep copy. When the CATs fall out of scope, their destructors are automatically invoked. The implementation of the CAT destructor is shown on lines 37–43. delete is called on both pointers, itsAge and itsWeight, returning the allocated memory to the free store. Also, for safety, the pointers are reassigned to NULL.

In this lesson, you learned how to overload member functions and how to write functions to support classes with dynamically allocated variables.

LESSON 17

OPERATOR OVERLOADING

In this lesson, you will learn how to overload member functions.

OPERATOR OVERLOADING

C++ has a number of built-in types, including int, float, double, and so forth. Each of these has a number of built-in operators, such as addition (+) and multiplication (*). C++ enables you to add these operators to your own classes as well.

In order to explore operator overloading fully, Listing 17.1 creates a new class, Counter. A Counter object will be used in counting (surprise!), in loops, and other applications where a number must be incremented, decremented, or otherwise tracked.

LISTING **17.1** THE Counter CLASS

```
1:      // Listing 17.1
2:      // The Counter class
3:
4:
5:      #include <iostream.h>
6:
7:      class Counter
8:      {
9:      public:
10:         Counter();
11:         ~Counter(){}
12:         int GetItsVal()const { return itsVal; }
13:         void SetItsVal(int x) {itsVal = x; }
14:
15:     private:
16:         int itsVal;
```

continues

LISTING 17.1   CONTINUED

```
17:
18:    };
19:
20:    Counter::Counter():
21:    itsVal(0)
22:    {};
23:
24:    int main()
25:    {
26:        Counter i;
27:        cout << "The value of i is ";
28:        cout << i.GetItsVal() << endl;
29:        return 0;
30:    }
```

The value of i is 0.

As it stands, this is a pretty useless class. It is defined on lines 7–18. Its only member variable is a int. The default constructor, which is declared on line 10 and whose implementation is on lines 20–22, initializes the one member variable, itsVal, to 0.

Unlike a real, built-in, honest, red-blooded int, the counter object cannot be incremented, decremented, added, assigned, or otherwise manipulated. In exchange for this, it makes printing its value far more difficult!

WRITING AN INCREMENT FUNCTION

Operator overloading restores much of the functionality that has been denied to user-defined classes such as Counter. Built-in classes have two increment operators, prefix (++x) and postfix (x++).

Before you can write the postfix operator, you must understand how it is different from the prefix operator. To review, prefix says *increment and then fetch,* whereas postfix says *fetch and then increment.*

Therefore, because the prefix operator can simply increment the value and then return the object itself, the postfix must return the value that existed before it was incremented. To do this, you must create a temporary object, after all. This temporary will hold the original value as you increment the value of the original object. You return the temporary, however, because the postfix operator asks for the original value, not the incremented value.

Let's go over that again. If you write

```
a = x++;
```

If x were 5, after this statement a is 5, but x is 6. This is because I returned the value in x and assigned it to a, and then increased the value of x. If x is an object, its postfix increment operator must stash away the original value (5) in a temporary object, increment x's value to 6, and then return that temporary to assign its value to a.

Note that because the temporary is being returned, it must be returned by value and not by reference, because the temporary will go out of scope as soon as the function returns.

You write the prefix operator as

```
const Counter& operator++ ();
```

You write the postfix operator as

```
const Counter& operator++ ();
```

This is indistinguishable from the prefix operator. By convention, an integer variable is supplied as a parameter to the operator declaration. The parameter's value is ignored; it's just a signal this is the postfix operator.

```
const Counter& operator++ (int flag);
```

Listing 17.2 demonstrates the use of both the prefix and the postfix operators.

Listing 17.2 PREFIX AND POSTFIX OPERATORS

```
1:      // Listing 17.2
2:      // Returning the dereferenced this pointer
3:
4:
5:      #include <iostream.h>
6:
7:      class Counter
8:      {
9:      public:
10:         Counter();
11:         ~Counter(){}
12:         int GetItsVal()const { return itsVal; }
```

continues

Listing 17.2 CONTINUED

```
13:        void SetItsVal(int x) {itsVal = x; }
14:        const Counter& operator++ ();        // prefix
15:        const Counter operator++ (int x);     // postfix
16:
17:    private:
18:        int itsVal;
19:    };
20:
21:    Counter::Counter():
22:    itsVal(0)
23:    {}
24:
25:    const Counter& Counter::operator++()
26:    {
27:        ++itsVal;
28:        return *this;
29:    }
30:
31:    const Counter Counter::operator++(int x)
32:    {
33:        Counter temp(*this);
34:        ++itsVal;
35:        return temp;
36:    }
37:
38:    int main()
39:    {
40:        Counter i;
41:        cout << "The value of i is ";
42:        cout << i.GetItsVal() << endl;
43:        i++;
44:        cout << "The value of i is ";
45:        cout << i.GetItsVal() << endl;
46:        ++i;
47:        cout << "The value of i is ";
48:        cout << i.GetItsVal() << endl;
49:        Counter a = ++i;
50:        cout << "The value of a: " << a.GetItsVal();
51:        cout << " and i: " << i.GetItsVal() << endl;
52:        a = i++;
53:        cout << "The value of a: " << a.GetItsVal();
54:        cout << " and i: " << i.GetItsVal() << endl;
55:        return 0;
56:    }
```

```
The value of i is 0
The value of i is 1
The value of i is 2
The value of a: 3 and i: 3
The value of a: 4 and i: 4
```

The postfix operator is declared on line 15 and implemented on lines 31–36. Note that the call to the prefix operator on line 14 does not include the flag integer (x), but is used with its normal syntax. The postfix operator uses a flag value (x) to signal it is the postfix and not the prefix. The flag value (x) is never used, however.

The implementation of the prefix operator++, on lines 25–29 returns a dereferenced this pointer. Thus, what is returned is the current, now incremented object. This provides a Counter object to be assigned to a. If the Counter object allocated memory, it would be important to override the copy constructor. In this case, the default copy constructor works fine.

Note that the value returned is a Counter reference, thereby avoiding the creation of an extra temporary object. It is a const reference because the value should not be changed by the function using this Counter.

Note also that on lines 31–36 the object makes a local copy of itself, increments itself, and then returns the unincremented copy. Thus, it meets the required semantics of fetch, then increment; what you get back is the unincremented value, but the object is left incremented.

operator+

The increment operator is a *unary* operator, which means that it operates on one object only. The addition operator (+) is a *binary* operator because two objects are involved. How do you implement overloading the + operator for Count?

The goal is to be able to declare two Counter variables and then add them, as in this example:

```
Counter varOne, varTwo, varThree;
VarThree = VarOne + VarTwo;
```

Overloading the + operator enables you to use this class as you would any built-in type.

Listing 17.3   operator+

```
1:      // Listing 17.3
2:      //Overload operator plus (+)
3:
4:
5:      #include <iostream.h>
6:
7:      class Counter
8:      {
9:      public:
10:         Counter();
11:         Counter(int initialValue);
12:         ~Counter(){}
13:         int GetItsVal()const { return itsVal; }
14:         void SetItsVal(int x) {itsVal = x; }
15:         Counter operator+ (const Counter &);
16:     private:
17:         int itsVal;
18:     };
19:
20:     Counter::Counter(int initialValue):
21:     itsVal(initialValue)
22:     {}
23:
24:     Counter::Counter():
25:     itsVal(0)
26:     {}
27:
28:     Counter Counter::operator+ (const Counter & rhs)
29:     {
30:         return Counter(itsVal + rhs.GetItsVal());
31:     }
32:
33:     int main()
34:     {
35:         Counter varOne(2), varTwo(4), varThree;
36:         varThree = varOne + varTwo;
37:         cout << "varOne: " << varOne.GetItsVal()<< endl;
38:         cout << "varTwo: " << varTwo.GetItsVal() << endl;
39:         cout << "varThree: " << varThree.GetItsVal();
40:         cout << endl;
41:
42:         return 0;
43:     }
```

```
varOne: 2
varTwo: 4
varThree: 6
```

operator+ is declared on line 15 and defined on lines 28–31. Note that a+b is translated by the compiler into a.operator+(b).

In this lesson, you learned how to overload operators.

LESSON 18

ADVANCED OPERATOR OVERLOADING

In this lesson, you will learn some of the limitations and dangers of over-loading operators and how to overcome them.

LIMITATIONS ON OPERATOR OVERLOADING

Operators on built-in types (such as `int`) cannot be overloaded. The precedence order cannot be changed, and the *arity* of the operator, that is, whether it is unary or binary, cannot be changed. You cannot make up new operators, so you cannot declare `**` to be the "power of" operator.

WHAT TO OVERLOAD

Operator overloading is one of the aspects of C++ most overused and abused by new programmers. It is tempting to create new and interesting uses for some of the more obscure operators, but these invariably lead to code that is confusing and difficult to read.

Of course, making the + operator subtract and the * operator add can be fun, but no professional programmer would do that. The greater danger lies in the well-intentioned but idiosyncratic use of an operator—using + to mean concatenate a series of letters, or / to mean split a string. There is good reason to consider these uses, but there is even better reason to proceed with caution. Remember, the goal of overloading operators is to increase usability and understanding.

operator=

You will remember that the compiler provides a default constructor, destructor, and copy constructor. The fourth and final function that is supplied by the compiler, if you don't specify one, is the assignment operator (operator=()).

This operator is called whenever you assign to an object. For example

```
class Cat
{
public:
    Cat (int age, weight);
    // ...
private:
    // ...
    int itsAge;
    int itsWeight;
};
CAT catOne(5,7);
CAT catTwo(3,4);
// ... other code here
catTwo = catOne;
```

Here, catOne is created and initialized with itsAge equal to 5 and itsWeight equal to 7. catTwo is then created and assigned the values 3 and 4.

No Copy Constructor   In this case, the copy constructor is not called. catTwo already exists; there is no need to construct it.

In Lesson 16, "Advanced Functions," I discussed the difference between a shallow or member-wise copy on the one hand, and a deep copy on the other. A shallow copy just copies the members, and both objects end up pointing to the same area on the free store. A deep copy allocates the necessary memory. You saw an illustration of that in Figure 16.1; refer back to that figure if you need to refresh your memory.

You see the same issue here with assignment as you did with the copy constructor. There is an added wrinkle with the assignment operator, however. The object catTwo already exists, and already has memory allocated.

If that memory is allocated on the heap (using operator new) then that
memory must be deleted if there is to be no memory leak.

So the first thing you must do when implementing the assignment operator is delete the memory assigned to its pointers. Note, if the allocated
memory is for a built in type (e.g., an int) and you are going to replace it
with a new value, rather than deleting and reallocating, you can just copy
the new value in place.

What happens if you assign catTwo to itself, like this:

```
catTwo = catTwo;
```

No one is likely to do this on purpose, but the program must be able to
handle it. More important, it is possible for this to happen by accident
when references and dereferenced pointers hide the fact the object's
assignment is to itself.

If you do not handle this problem carefully, catTwo deletes its memory
allocation. Then, when it is ready to copy in the memory from the right-
hand side of the assignment, it has a very big problem: the memory is
gone.

To protect against this, your assignment operator must check to see if the
right-hand side of the assignment operator is the object itself. It does this
by examining the this pointer. Listing 18.1 shows a class with an assignment operator.

Listing 18.1   AN ASSIGNMENT OPERATOR

```
1:      // Listing 18.1
2:      // Assignment Operator
3:
4:      #include <iostream.h>
5:
6:      class CAT
7:      {
8:      public:
9:         CAT(); // default constructor
10:        // copy constructor and destructor elided!
11:        int GetAge() const { return *itsAge; }
12:        int GetWeight() const { return *itsWeight; }
13:        void SetAge(int age) { *itsAge = age; }
14:        CAT operator=(const CAT &);
15:
```

```
16:      private:
17:          int *itsAge;
18:          int *itsWeight;
19:      };
20:
21:      CAT::CAT()
22:      {
23:          itsAge = new int;
24:          itsWeight = new int;
25:          *itsAge = 5;
26:          *itsWeight = 9;
27:      }
28:
29:
30:      CAT CAT::operator=(const CAT & rhs)
31:      {
32:          if (this == &rhs)
33:              return *this;
38:          *itsAge = rhs.GetAge();
39:          *itsWeight = rhs.GetWeight();
40:          return *this;
41:      }
42:
43:
44:      int main()
45:      {
46:          CAT frisky;
47:          cout << "frisky's age: " << frisky.GetAge()
               ➥<< endl;
48:          cout << "Setting frisky to 6...\n";
49:          frisky.SetAge(6);
50:          CAT whiskers;
51:          cout << "whiskers' age: " <<
               ➥ whiskers.GetAge() << endl;
52:          cout << "copying frisky to whiskers...\n";
53:          whiskers = frisky;
54:          cout << "whiskers' age: " <<
               ➥ whiskers.GetAge() << endl;
55:          return 0;
56:      }
```

```
frisky's age: 5
Setting frisky to 6;
whiskers' age: 5
copying frisky to whiskers...
whiskers' age: 6
```

Listing 18.1 creates a CAT class, and leaves out the copy constructor and destructor to save room. On line 14, the assignment operator is declared; and on lines 30–41, it is defined.

On line 32, the current object (the CAT being assigned to) is tested to see if it is the same as the CAT being assigned. This is done by checking if the address of rhs is the same as the address stored in the this pointer. An alternative test is to dereference the this pointer and see if the two objects are the same:

```
if (*this == rhs)
```

Of course, the equality operator (==) can be overloaded as well, enabling you to determine for yourself what it means for your objects to be equal.

CONVERSION OPERATORS

What happens when you try to assign a variable of a built-in type, such as int or unsigned short, to an object of a user-defined class? Listing 18.2 brings back the Counter class and attempts to assign a variable of type int to a Counter object.

 Caution Listing 18.2 will not compile!

Listing 18.2 ATTEMPTING TO ASSIGN AN INT TO A COUNTER

```
1:      // Listing 18.2
2:      // This code won't compile!
3:
4:
5:      #include <iostream.h>
6:
7:      class Counter
8:      {
9:      public:
10:         Counter();
11:         ~Counter(){}
12:         int GetItsVal()const { return itsVal; }
13:         void SetItsVal(int x) {itsVal = x; }
14:     private:
15:         int itsVal;
```

```
16:
17:     };
18:
19:     Counter::Counter():
20:     itsVal(0)
21:     {}
22:
23:     int main()
24:     {
25:         int theShort = 5;
26:         Counter theCtr = theShort;
27:         cout << "theCtr: " << theCtr.GetItsVal() << endl;
28:          return 0;
29:     }
```

```
Compiler error! Unable to convert int to Counter
```

OUTPUT

The Counter class declared on lines 7–17 has only a default constructor. It declares no particular method for turning an int into a Counter object, so line 26 causes a compile error. The compiler cannot figure out, unless you tell it, that given an int it should assign that value to the member variable itsVal.

Listing 18.3 corrects this by creating a conversion operator: a constructor that takes an int and produces a Counter object.

Listing 18.3   CONVERTING int TO Counter

```
1:      // Listing 18.3
2:      // Constructor as conversion operator
3:
4:
5:      #include <iostream.h>
6:
7:      class Counter
8:      {
9:      public:
10:         Counter();
11:         Counter(int val);
12:         ~Counter(){}
13:         int GetItsVal()const { return itsVal; }
14:         void SetItsVal(int x) {itsVal = x; }
15:      private:
16:         int itsVal;
17:
```

continues

Listing 18.3 CONTINUED

```
18:     };
19:
20:     Counter::Counter():
21:     itsVal(0)
22:     {}
23:
24:     Counter::Counter(int val):
25:     itsVal(val)
26:     {}
27:
28:
29:     int main()
30:     {
31:         int theShort = 5;
32:         Counter theCtr = theShort;
33:         cout << "theCtr: " << theCtr.GetItsVal() << endl;
34:         return 0;
35:     }
```

OUTPUT

theCtr: 5

The important change is on line 11, where the constructor is overloaded to take a int, and on lines 24–26, where the constructor is implemented. The effect of this constructor is to create a Counter out of an int.

Given this, the compiler is able to call the constructor that takes an int as its argument. What happens, however, if you try to reverse the assignment with the following?

```
1:   Counter theCtr(5);
2:   int theShort = theCtr;
3:   cout << "theShort : " << theShort  << endl;
```

Again, this will generate a compile error. Although the compiler now knows how to create a Counter out of an int, it does not know how to reverse the process.

THE unsigned short() OPERATOR

To solve this and similar problems, C++ provides conversion operators that can be added to your class. This enables your class to specify how to do implicit conversions to built-in types. Listing 18.4 illustrates this.

No Return Value   Conversion operators do not specify a return value, even though they do, in effect, return a converted value.

Listing 18.4   CONVERTING FROM Counter TO unsigned short()

```
1:   // Listing 18.4
2:   // conversion operator
3:
4:   #include <iostream.h>
5:
6:   class Counter
7:   {
8:   public:
9:       Counter();
10:       Counter(int val);
11:       ~Counter(){}
12:       int GetItsVal()const { return itsVal; }
13:       void SetItsVal(int x) {itsVal = x; }
14:       operator int();
15:  private:
16:       int itsVal;
17:
18:  };
19:
20:  Counter::Counter():
21:  itsVal(0)
22:  {}
23:
24:  Counter::Counter(int val):
25:  itsVal(val)
26:  {}
27:
28:  Counter::operator int ()
29:  {
30:      return ( int (itsVal) );
31:  }
32:
33:  int main()
34:  {
35:      Counter ctr(5);
36:      int theInt = ctr;
37:      cout << " theInt: " << theInt << endl;
38:      return 0;
39:  }
```

theShort: 5

On line 14, the conversion operator is declared. Note that it has no return value. The implementation of this function is on lines 28–31. Line 30 returns the value of itsVal converted to an int.

Now the compiler knows how to turn ints into Counter objects and vice versa, and they can be assigned to one another freely.

In this, lesson you learned how to work with operator overloading effectively.

LESSON 19

ARRAYS

In this lesson, you will learn what arrays are and how to declare them.

WHAT IS AN ARRAY?

An *array* is a collection of data storage locations, each of which holds the same type of data. Each storage location is called an element of the array.

You declare an array by writing the type, followed by the array name and the subscript.

 Subscript   The number of elements in the array, surrounded by square brackets.

For example,

```
long LongArray[25];
```

declares an array of 25 `long` integers, named `LongArray`. When the compiler sees this declaration, it sets aside enough memory to hold all 25 elements. Because each `long` integer requires 4 bytes, this declaration sets aside 100 contiguous bytes of memory, as illustrated in Figure 19.1.

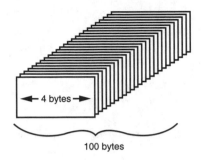

Figure 19.1   Declaring an array.

ARRAY ELEMENTS

You access each of the array elements by referring to an offset from the array name. Array elements are counted from 0; therefore, the first array element is arrayName[0]. In the LongArray example, LongArray[0] is the first array element, LongArray[1] the second, and so forth.

This can be somewhat confusing. The array SomeArray[3] has three elements: SomeArray[0], SomeArray[1], and SomeArray[2]. More generally, SomeArray[n] has n elements that are numbered SomeArray[0] through SomeArray[n-1].

Therefore, LongArray[25] is numbered from LongArray[0] through LongArray[24]. Listing 19.1 shows how to declare an array of five integers and fill each with a value.

Listing 19.1   USING AN INTEGER ARRAY

```
1:      //Listing 19.1 - Arrays
2:      #include <iostream.h>
3:
4:      int main()
5:      {
6:          int myArray[5];
7           int i;
8:          for (i=0; i<5; i++)   // 0-4
9:          {
10:             cout << "Value for myArray[" << i << "]: ";
11:             cin >> myArray[i];
```

```
12:        }
13:        for (i = 0; i<5; i++)
14:            cout << i << ": " << myArray[i] << "\n";
15:        return 0;
16:    }
```

```
Value for myArray[0]:   3
Value for myArray[1]:   6
Value for myArray[2]:   9
Value for myArray[3]:   12
Value for myArray[4]:   15

0: 3
1: 6
2: 9
3: 12
4: 15
```

Line 6 declares an array called myArray, which holds five integer variables. Line 8 establishes a loop that counts from 0 through 4, which is the proper set of offsets for a five-element array. The user is prompted for a value, and that value is saved at the correct offset into the array.

The first value is saved at myArray[0], the second at myArray[1], and so forth. The second for loop prints each value to the screen.

How Arrays Count   Arrays count from 0, not from 1. This is the cause of many bugs in programs written by C++ novices. Whenever you use an array, remember an array with 10 elements counts from ArrayName[0] to ArrayName[9]. There is no ArrayName[10].

WRITING PAST THE END OF AN ARRAY

When you write a value to an element in an array, the compiler computes where to store the value based on the size of each element and the subscript. Suppose that you ask to write over the value at LongArray[5], which is the sixth element. The compiler multiplies the offset (5) by the size of each element, in this case, 4. It then moves that many bytes (20) from the beginning of the array and writes the new value at that location.

If you ask to write at `LongArray[50]`, the compiler ignores the fact that there is no such element. It computes how far past the first element it should look—200 bytes—and then writes over whatever is at that location. This can be virtually any data, and writing your new value there might have unpredictable results. If you're lucky, your program will crash immediately. If you're unlucky, you'll get strange results much later in your program, and you'll have a difficult time figuring out what went wrong.

FENCE POST ERRORS

It is so common to write to one past the end of an array that this bug has its own name. It is called a *fence post error*. This refers to the problem of counting how many fence posts you need for a 10-foot fence if you need one post for every foot. Most people answer 10, but of course you need 11. Figure 19.2 makes this clear.

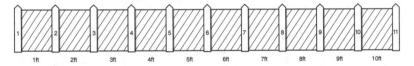

Figure 19.2   Fence post errors.

This sort of "off by one" counting can be the bane of any programmer's life. In time, however, you'll get used to the idea that a 25-element array counts only to element 24, and everything counts from 0. (Programmers wonder why office buildings don't have a floor zero. Indeed, some programmers have been known to push the 4 elevator button when they want to get to the fifth floor.)

INITIALIZING ARRAYS

You can initialize a simple array of built-in types, such as integers and characters, when you first declare the array. After the array name, you put an equal sign (=) and a list of comma-separated values enclosed in braces. For example

```
int IntegerArray[5] = { 10, 20, 30, 40, 50 };
```

declares `IntegerArray` to be an array of five integers. It assigns `IntegerArray[0]` the value 10, `IntegerArray[1]` the value 20, and so forth.

If you omit the size of the array, an array just big enough to hold the initialization is created. Therefore, if you write

```
int IntegerArray[] = { 10, 20, 30, 40, 50 };
```

you will create exactly the same array as you did in the previous example.

If you need to know the size of the array, you can ask the compiler to compute it for you. For example

```
const int IntegerArrayLength =

      sizeof(IntegerArray)/sizeof(IntegerArray[0]);
```

sets the constant `int` variable `IntegerArrayLength` to the result obtained from dividing the size of the entire array by the size of each individual entry in the array. That quotient is the number of members in the array.

ARRAYS OF OBJECTS

Any object, whether built-in or user defined, can be stored in an array. When you declare the array, you tell the compiler the type of object to store and the number of objects for which to allocate room. The compiler knows how much room is needed for each object based on the class declaration. The class must have a default constructor that takes no arguments so the objects can be created when the array is defined.

Accessing member data in an array of objects is a two-step process. You identify the member of the array by using the index operator ([ ]), and then you add the member operator (.) to access the particular member variable.

ARRAYS OF POINTERS

The arrays discussed so far store all their members on the stack. Usually stack memory is severely limited, whereas free store memory is far larger.

It is possible to declare each object on the free store and then to store only a pointer to the object in the array. This dramatically reduces the amount of stack memory used. Listing 19.2 rewrites the array but stores all the objects on the free store. As an indication of the greater memory now available, the array is expanded from 5 to 500, and the name is changed from Litter to Family.

Listing 19.2   STORING AN ARRAY ON THE FREE STORE

```
1:      // Listing 19.2 - An array of pointers to objects
2:
3:      #include <iostream.h>
4:
5:      class CAT
6:      {
7:      public:
8:          CAT() { itsAge = 1; itsWeight=5; }
9:          ~CAT() {}
10:         int GetAge() const { return itsAge; }
11:         int GetWeight() const { return itsWeight; }
12:         void SetAge(int age) { itsAge = age; }
13:
14:     private:
15:         int itsAge;
16:         int itsWeight;
17:     };
18:
19:     int main()
20:     {
21:         CAT * Family[500];
22:         int i;
23:         CAT * pCat;
24:         for (i = 0; i < 500; i++)
25:         {
26:             pCat = new CAT;
27:             pCat->SetAge(2*i +1);
28:             Family[i] = pCat;
29:         }
30:
31:         for (i = 0; i < 500; i++)
32:             cout << "Cat #" << i+1 << ": ";
33:             cout << Family[i]->GetAge() << endl;
34:         return 0;
35:     }
```

```
Cat #1: 1
Cat #2: 3
Cat #3: 5
...
Cat #499: 997
Cat #500: 999
```

In the initial loop (lines 24–29), 500 new CAT objects are created on the free store, and each one has its age set to twice the index plus one. Therefore, the first CAT is set to 1, the second CAT to 3, the third CAT to 5, and so on. Finally, the pointer is added to the array.

Because the array has been declared to hold pointers, the pointer—rather than the dereferenced value in the pointer—is added to the array.

The second loop (lines 31 and 32) prints each of the values. The pointer is accessed by using the index, Family[i]. That address is then used to access the GetAge() method.

In this example, the array Family and all its pointers are stored on the stack, but the 500 CATs that are created are stored on the free store. In this simple example, we don't delete these objects because the program ends, but you do want to be careful to free this memory in a "real" program to avoid the problem of memory leaks.

DECLARING ARRAYS ON THE FREE STORE

It is possible to put the entire array on the free store, also known as the *heap*. You do this by calling new and using the subscript operator. The result is a pointer to an area on the free store that holds the array. For example

```
CAT *Family = new CAT[500];
```

declares Family to be a pointer to the first in an array of 500 CATs. In other words, Family points to (or has the address of) Family[0].

The advantage of using Family in this way is that you can use pointer arithmetic to access each member of Family. For example you can write:

```
CAT *Family = new CAT[500];
CAT *pCat = Family;              // pCat points to Family[0]

pCat->SetAge(10);               // set Family[0] to 10
pCat++;                         // advance to Family[1]
pCat->SetAge(20);               // set Family[1] to 20
```

This declares a new array of 500 CATs and a pointer to point to the start of the array. Using that pointer, the first CAT's SetAge() function is called with the value 10. The pointer is then incremented to point to the next CAT, and the second CAT's SetAge() method is then called.

A POINTER TO AN ARRAY VERSUS AN ARRAY OF POINTERS

Examine these three declarations:

```
1:  Cat    FamilyOne[500]
2:  CAT * FamilyTwo[500];
3:  CAT * FamilyThree = new CAT[500];
```

FamilyOne is an array of 500 CATs. FamilyTwo is an array of 500 pointers to CATs. FamilyThree is a pointer to an array of 500 CATs.

The differences among these three code lines dramatically affect how these arrays operate. What is perhaps even more surprising is that FamilyThree is a variant of FamilyOne, but is very different from FamilyTwo.

This raises the thorny issue of how pointers relate to arrays. In the third case, FamilyThree is a pointer to an array. That is, the address in FamilyThree is the address of the first item in that array. This is exactly the case for FamilyOne.

POINTERS AND ARRAY NAMES

In C++, an array name is a constant pointer to the first element of the array. Therefore, in the declaration

```
CAT Family[50];
```

`Family` is a pointer to `&Family[0]`, which is the address of the first element of the array `Family`.

It is legal to use array names as constant pointers, and vice versa. Therefore, `Family + 4` is a legitimate way of accessing the data at `Family[4]`.

The compiler does all the arithmetic when you add to, increment, and decrement pointers. The address accessed when you write `Family + 4` isn't 4 bytes past the address of `Family`—it is four objects. If each object is 4 bytes long, `Family + 4` is 16 bytes. If each object is a `CAT` that has four `long` member variables of 4 bytes each and two `short` member variables of 2 bytes each, each `CAT` is 20 bytes, and `Family + 4` is 80 bytes past the start of the array.

Listing 19.3 illustrates declaring and using an array on the free store.

Listing 19.3 CREATING AN ARRAY BY USING new

```
1:      // Listing 19.3 - An array on the free store
2:
3:      #include <iostream.h>
4:
5:      class CAT
6:      {
7:      public:
8:          CAT() { itsAge = 1; itsWeight=5; }
9:          ~CAT();
10:         int GetAge() const { return itsAge; }
11:         int GetWeight() const { return itsWeight; }
12:         void SetAge(int age) { itsAge = age; }
13:
14:     private:
15:         int itsAge;
16:         int itsWeight;
17:     };
18:
19:     CAT :: ~CAT()
20:     {
21:        // cout << "Destructor called!\n";
22:     }
23:
24:     int main()
25:     {
```

continues

Listing 19.3 CONTINUED

```
26:        CAT * Family = new CAT[500];
27:        int i;
28:        CAT * pCat;
29:        for (i = 0; i < 500; i++)
30:        {
31:            pCat = new CAT;
32:            pCat->SetAge(2*i +1);
33:            Family[i] = *pCat;
34:            delete pCat;
35:        }
36:
37:        for (i = 0; i < 500; i++)
38:        {
39:            cout << "Cat #" << i+1 << ": ";
40:            cout << Family[i].GetAge() << endl;
41:        }
42:
43:        delete [] Family;
44:
45:        return 0;
46:    }
```

OUTPUT

```
Cat #1: 1
Cat #2: 3
Cat #3: 5
...
Cat #499: 997
Cat #500: 999
```

Line 26 declares the array Family, which holds 500 CAT objects. The entire array is created on the free store with the call to new CAT[500].

Each CAT object added to the array also is created on the free store (line 31). Note, however, the pointer isn't added to the array this time; the object itself is. This array isn't an array of pointers to CATs—it is an array of CATs.

DELETING ARRAYS ON THE FREE STORE

Family is a pointer to the array on the free store. When, on line 33, the pointer pCat is dereferenced, the CAT object itself is stored in the array (why not? the array is on the free store). But pCat is used again in the next iteration of the loop. Is there a danger there will now be no pointer to that CAT object, and a memory leak has been created?

This would be a big problem, except that deleting Family returns all the memory set aside for the array. The compiler is smart enough to destroy each object in the array and to return its memory to the free store.

To see this, change the size of the array from 500 to 10 in lines 26, 29, and 37. Then uncomment the cout statement in line 21. When line 40 is reached and the array is destroyed, each CAT object destructor is called.

When you create an item on the heap by using new, you always delete that item and free its memory with delete. Similarly, when you create an array by using new <class>[size], you delete that array and free all its memory with delete[]. The brackets signal to the compiler that this array is being deleted.

If you leave the brackets off, only the first object in the array will be deleted. You can prove this to yourself by removing the brackets on line 40. If you edited line 21 so the destructor prints, you should then see only one CAT object destroyed. Congratulations! You just created a memory leak.

In this lesson, you learned how to create and manipulate arrays.

LESSON 20

CHARACTER ARRAYS

In this lesson, you will learn what strings are and how to use character arrays to make them.

char ARRAYS

The only strings you've seen until now have been unnamed string constants used in cout statements, such as

```
cout << "hello world.\n";
```

In C++, a string is an array of chars ending with a null character. You can declare and initialize a string just as you would any other array. For example:

```
char Greeting[] =

    { 'H', 'e', 'l', 'l', 'o', ' ', 'W','o','r','l','d', '\0' };
```

The last character, '\0', is the null character, which many C++ functions recognize as the terminator for a string.

 String   A series of characters.

Although this character-by-character approach works, it is difficult to type and admits too many opportunities for error. C++ enables you to use a shorthand form of the previous line of code:

```
char Greeting[] = "Hello World";
```

You should note two things about this syntax:

- Instead of single quoted characters separated by commas and surrounded by braces, you have a double-quoted string, no commas, and no braces.

- You don't need to add the null character because the compiler adds it for you.

The string `Hello World` is 12 bytes: `Hello` is 5 bytes, the space is 1, `World` is 5, and the null character is 1 byte.

You can also create uninitialized character arrays. As with all arrays, it is important to ensure that you don't put more into the buffer than there is room for.

Listing 20.1 demonstrates the use of an uninitialized buffer.

Listing 20.1 FILLING AN ARRAY

```
1:     //Listing 20.1 char array buffers
2:
3:     #include <iostream.h>
4:
5:     int main()
6:     {
7:         char buffer[80];
8:         cout << "Enter the string: ";
9:         cin >> buffer;
10:        cout << "Here's the buffer:  " << buffer << endl;
11:        return 0;
12:    }
```

```
Enter the string: Hello World
Here's the buffer: Hello
```

OUTPUT

On line 7 a buffer is declared to hold 80 characters. This is large enough to hold a 79-character string and a terminating null character.

On line 8 the user is prompted to enter a string, which is entered into the buffer on line 9. It is the syntax of `cin` to write a terminating null to the buffer after it writes the string.

There are two problems with the program in Listing 20.1. First, if the user enters more than 79 characters, `cin` writes past the end of the buffer. Second, if the user enters a space, `cin` thinks that it is the end of the string, and it stops writing to the buffer.

To solve these problems, you must call a special method on cin: get().
Cin.get() takes three parameters:

- The buffer to fill

- The maximum number of characters to get

- The delimiter that terminates input

The default delimiter is newline. Listing 20.2 illustrates its use.

Listing 20.2   FILLING AN ARRAY
```
1:      //Listing 20.2 using cin.get()
2:
3:      #include <iostream.h>
4:
5:      int main()
6:      {
7:          char buffer[80];
8:          cout << "Enter the string: ";
            ➥// get up to 79 or newline
9:          cin.get(buffer, 79);
10:         cout << "Here's the buffer:  " << buffer << endl;
11:         return 0;
12:     }
```

OUTPUT

```
Enter the string: Hello World
Here's the buffer: Hello World
```

Line 9 calls the method get() of cin. The buffer declared in line 7 is
passed in as the first argument. The second argument is the maximum
number of characters to get. In this case, it must be 79 to allow for the terminating null. There is no need to provide a terminating character because
the default value of newline is sufficient.

strcpy() AND strncpy()

C++ inherits from C a library of functions for dealing with strings.
Among the many functions provided are two for copying one string into
another: strcpy() and strncpy(). strcpy() copies the entire contents of
one string into a designated buffer. Listing 20.3 demonstrates its use.

Listing 20.3   Using strcpy()

```
1:      #include <iostream.h>
2:      #include <string.h>
3:      int main()
4:      {
5:          char String1[] = "No man is an island";
6:          char String2[80];
7:
8:          strcpy(String2,String1);
9:
10:         cout << "String1: " << String1 << endl;
11:         cout << "String2: " << String2 << endl;
12:         return 0;
13:     }
```

```
String1: No man is an island
String2: No man is an island
```

The header file STRING.H is included in line 2. This file contains the prototype of the strcpy() function. strcpy() takes two character arrays—a destination followed by a source. If the source were larger than the destination, strcpy() would overwrite past the end of the buffer.

To protect against this, the standard library also includes strncpy(). This variation takes a maximum number of characters to copy. strncpy() copies up to the first null character or the maximum number of characters specified into the destination buffer.

Listing 20.4 illustrates the use of strncpy().

Listing 20.4   Using strncpy()

```
1:      #include <iostream.h>
2:      #include <string.h>
3:      int main()
4:      {
5:          const int MaxLength = 80;
6:          char String1[] = "No man is an island";
7:          char String2[MaxLength+1];
8:
9:
10:         strncpy(String2,String1,MaxLength);
11:         String2[strlen(String1)] = '\0';
12:         cout << "String1: " << String1 << endl;
13:         cout << "String2: " << String2 << endl;
14:         return 0;
15:     }
```

OUTPUT

```
String1: No man is an island
String2: No man is an island
```

In line 10, the call to `strcpy()` has been changed to a call to `strncpy()`, which takes a third parameter: the maximum number of characters to copy. The buffer `String2` is declared to take `MaxLength+1` characters. The extra character is for the null, which must terminate the string.

STRING CLASSES

Modern C++ compilers come with a class library that includes a large set of classes for data manipulation. The standard library now includes an object-oriented string class.

C++ inherited the null-terminated string and the library of functions that includes `strcpy()` from C, but these functions aren't integrated into an object-oriented framework. The `String` class provides an encapsulated set of data and functions for manipulating that data, as well as accessor functions so that the data itself is hidden from the clients of the `String` class.

In this lesson you learned how arrays of characters can be manipulated as "strings."

LESSON 21

INHERITANCE

In this lesson, you will learn how C++ captures one very important relationship: specialization/generalization.

WHAT IS INHERITANCE?

What exactly does it mean when I say something is a kind of something else? I mean that it is a specialization of that thing. That is, a dog is a special kind of mammal. Dogs and horses are both mammals; they are distinguished by their specific characteristics of "dog-ness" or "horse-ness," but to the extent they are mammals; they are identical. Their "mammal-ness" is shared.

C++ attempts to represent these relationships by enabling you to define classes that derive from one another. Derivation is a way of expressing the *is-a* relationship. You derive a new class, dog, from the class mammal.

A class which adds new functionality to an existing class is said to derive from that original class. The original class is said to be the new class's base class.

Typically, a base class will have more than one derived class. Just as dogs, cats, and horses are all types of mammals, their classes would all derive from the mammal class.

THE SYNTAX OF DERIVATION

When you declare a class, you indicate what class it derives from by writing a colon after the class name, the type of derivation (public or otherwise), and the class from which it derives. The following is an example:

```
class Dog : public Mammal
```

Public and Private Inheritance   There is both public and private inheritance, but private inheritance is beyond the scope of this book. Always use public inheritance to model specialization.

The class from which you derive must have been declared earlier, or you will get a compiler error. Listing 21.1 illustrates how to declare a Dog class that is derived from a Mammal class.

Listing 21.1 SIMPLE INHERITANCE

```
1:      //Listing 21.1 Simple inheritance
2:
3:      #include <iostream.h>
4:      enum BREED
5:      {
6:          YORKIE, CAIRN, DANDIE, SHETLAND, DOBERMAN, LAB
7:      };
8:
9:      class Mammal
10:      {
11:      public:
12          // constructors
13:         Mammal();
14:         ~Mammal();
15:
16:         //accessors
17:         int GetAge()const;
18:         void SetAge(int);
19:         int GetWeight() const;
20:         void SetWeight();
21:
22:         //Other methods
23:         void Speak() const;
24:         void Sleep() const;
25:
26:
27:      protected:
28:          int itsAge;
29:          int itsWeight;
30:      };
31:
32:      class Dog : public Mammal
```

```
33:      {
34:      public:
35:
36:          // Constructors
37:          Dog();
38:          ~Dog();
39:
40:          // Accessors
41:          BREED GetBreed() const;
42:          void SetBreed(BREED);
43:
44:          // Other methods
45:          WagTail() const;
46:          BegForFood() const;
47:
48:      protected:
49:          BREED itsBreed;
50:      };
```

This program has no output because it is only a set of class declarations without their implementations. Nonetheless, there is much to see here.

On lines 9–30, the Mammal class is declared. Note that in this example, Mammal does not derive from any other class. In the real world, mammals do derive, that is, mammals are kinds of animals. In a C++ program, you can represent only a fraction of the information you have about any given object. Reality is far too complex to capture it all, so every C++ hierarchy is an arbitrary representation of the data available. The trick of a good design is to represent the areas that you care about in a way that maps back to reality in a reasonably faithful way.

The hierarchy has to begin somewhere; this program begins with Mammal. Because of this decision, some member variables that might properly belong in a higher base class are now represented here. For example, certainly all animals have an age and weight, so if Mammal derived from Animal you might expect to inherit those attributes. As it is, the attributes appear in the Mammal class.

To keep the program reasonably simple and manageable, only six methods have been put in the Mammal class—four accessor methods, Speak(), and Sleep().

The Dog class inherits from Mammal, as indicated on line 32. Every Dog object will have three member variables: itsAge, itsWeight, and itsBreed. Note that the class declaration for Dog does not include the member variables itsAge and itsWeight. Dog objects inherit these variables from the Mammal class, along with all Mammal's methods except the copy operator, the constructors, and the destructor.

PRIVATE VERSUS PROTECTED MEMBERS

You may have noticed that a new access keyword, protected, has been introduced on lines 27 and 48 of Listing 21.1. Previously, class data was declared private. However, private members are not available to derived classes. You could make itsAge and itsWeight public, but that is not desirable. You don't want other classes accessing these data members directly.

What you want is a designation that says, "Make these visible to this class and to classes that derive from this class." That designation is protected. Protected data members and functions are fully visible to derived classes, but are otherwise private.

There are, in total, three access specifiers: public, protected, and private. If a function has an object of your class, it can access all the public member data and functions. The member functions, in turn, can access all private data members and functions of their own class, and all protected data members and functions of any class from which they derive.

Therefore, the function Dog::WagTail() can access the private data itsBreed and can access the protected data in the Mammal class.

Even if other classes are layered between Mammal and Dog (for example, DomesticAnimals) the Dog class will still be able to access the protected members of Mammal, assuming that these other classes all use public inheritance.

Listing 21.2 demonstrates how to create objects of type Dog and access the data and functions of that type.

LISTING 21.2   USING A DERIVED OBJECT

```
1:      //Listing 21.2 Using a derived object
2:
3:      #include <iostream.h>
4:      enum BREED { YORKIE, CAIRN, DANDIE,
        ➥ SHETLAND, DOBERMAN, LAB };
5:
6:      class Mammal
7:      {
8:      public:
9:          // constructors
10:         Mammal():itsAge(2), itsWeight(5){}
11:         ~Mammal(){}
12:
13:         //accessors
14:         int GetAge()const { return itsAge; }
15:         void SetAge(int age) { itsAge = age; }
16:         int GetWeight() const { return itsWeight; }
17:         void SetWeight(int weight) { itsWeight = weight; }
18:
19:         //Other methods
20:         void Speak() const { cout << "Mammal sound!\n"; }
21:         void Sleep() const
22:            { cout << "shhh. I'm sleeping.\n"; }
23:
24:
25:      protected:
26:         int itsAge;
27:         int itsWeight;
28:      };
29:
30:      class Dog : public Mammal
31:      {
32:      public:
33:
34:         // Constructors
35:         Dog():itsBreed(YORKIE){}
36:         ~Dog(){}
37:
38:         // Accessors
39:         BREED GetBreed() const { return itsBreed; }
40:         void SetBreed(BREED breed) { itsBreed = breed; }
41:
42:         // Other methods
43:         void WagTail() const
```

continues

LISTING 21.2 CONTINUED

```
44:            { cout << "Tail wagging...\n"; }
45:         void BegForFood() const
46:            { cout << "Begging for food...\n"; }
47:
48:      private:
49:         BREED itsBreed;
50:      };
51:
52:      int main()
53:      {
54:         Dog fido;
55:         fido.Speak();
56:         fido.WagTail();
57:         cout << "Fido is " << fido.GetAge();
58:         cout << " years old\n";
59:      return 0;
60:      }
```

```
Mammal sound!
Tail wagging...
Fido is 2 years old
```

OUTPUT

On lines 6–28, the Mammal class is declared (all its functions are inline to save space here). On lines 30–50, the Dog class is declared as a derived class of Mammal. Thus, by these declarations, all Dogs have an age, a weight, and a breed.

On line 54 a Dog is declared, Fido. Fido inherits all the attributes of a Mammal, as well as all the attributes of a Dog. Thus Fido knows how to WagTail(), but also knows how to Speak() and Sleep().

In this lesson, you learned how to use inheritance to model specialization and generalization.

Lesson 22

Issues in Inheritance

In this lesson, you will learn how to manage the issues raised by inheritance.

Constructors and Destructors

Dog objects are Mammal objects. This is the essence of the *is-a* relationship. When Fido is created, his base constructor is called first, creating a Mammal. Then the Dog constructor is called, completing the construction of the Dog object. Because you gave Fido no parameters, the default constructor was called in each case. Fido doesn't exist until he is completely constructed, which means that both his Mammal part and his Dog part must be constructed. Thus, both constructors must be called.

When Fido is destroyed, first the Dog destructor will be called, and then the destructor for the Mammal part of Fido. Each destructor is given an opportunity to clean up after its own part of Fido. Remember to clean up after your Dog!

Passing Arguments to Base Constructors

It is possible you'll want to overload the constructor of Mammal to take a specific age, and you'll want to overload the Dog constructor to take a breed. How do you get the age and weight parameters passed up to the right constructor in Mammal? What if Dogs want to initialize weight but Mammals don't?

Base class initialization can be performed during class initialization by writing the base class name, followed by the parameters expected by the base class. Listing 22.1 demonstrates this.

LISTING 22.1   OVERLOADING CONSTRUCTORS IN DERIVED CLASSES

```
1:      //Listing 22.1 Overloading constructors
2:
3:      #include <iostream.h>
4:      enum BREED
5:      {
6:         YORKIE, CAIRN, DANDIE, SHETLAND, DOBERMAN, LAB
7:      };
8:
9:      class Mammal
10:      {
11:      public:
12:          // constructors
13:          Mammal();
14:          Mammal(int age);
15:          ~Mammal();
16:
17:          //accessors
18:          int GetAge() const { return itsAge; }
19:          void SetAge(int age) { itsAge = age; }
20:          int GetWeight() const { return itsWeight; }
21:          void SetWeight(int weight)
22:             { itsWeight = weight; }
23:
24:          //Other methods
25:          void Speak() const { cout << "Mammal sound!\n"; }
26:          void Sleep() const
27:             { cout << "shhh. I'm sleeping.\n"; }
28:
29:
30:      protected:
31:          int itsAge;
32:          int itsWeight;
33:      };
34:
35:      class Dog : public Mammal
36:      {
37:      public:
38:
39:          // Constructors
40:          Dog();
41:          Dog(int age);
42:          Dog(int age, int weight);
43:          Dog(int age, BREED breed);
44:          Dog(int age, int weight, BREED breed);
45:          ~Dog();
46:
```

```
47:        // Accessors
48:        BREED GetBreed() const { return itsBreed; }
49:        void SetBreed(BREED breed) { itsBreed = breed; }
50:
51:        // Other methods
52:        void WagTail() const
53:            { cout << "Tail wagging...\n"; }
54:        void BegForFood() const
55:            { cout << "Begging for food...\n"; }
56:
57:    private:
58:        BREED itsBreed;
59:    };
60:
61:    Mammal::Mammal():
62:    itsAge(1),
63:    itsWeight(5)
64:    {
65:        cout << "Mammal constructor...\n";
66:    }
67:
68:    Mammal::Mammal(int age):
69:    itsAge(age),
70:    itsWeight(5)
71:    {
72:        cout << "Mammal(int) constructor...\n";
73:    }
74:
75:    Mammal::~Mammal()
76:    {
77:        cout << "Mammal destructor...\n";
78:    }
79:
80:    Dog::Dog():
81:    Mammal(),
82:    itsBreed(YORKIE)
83:    {
84:        cout << "Dog constructor...\n";
85:    }
86:
87:    Dog::Dog(int age):
88:    Mammal(age),
89:    itsBreed(YORKIE)
90:    {
91:        cout << "Dog(int) constructor...\n";
```

continues

LISTING 22.1   CONTINUED

```
92:    }
93:
94:    Dog::Dog(int age, int weight):
95:    Mammal(age),
96:    itsBreed(YORKIE)
97:    {
98:        itsWeight = weight;
99:        cout << "Dog(int, int) constructor...\n";
100:    }
101:
102:    Dog::Dog(int age, int weight, BREED breed):
103:    Mammal(age),
104:    itsBreed(breed)
105:    {
106:        itsWeight = weight;
107:        cout << "Dog(int, int, BREED) constructor...\n";
108:    }
109:
110:    Dog::Dog(int age, BREED breed):
111:    Mammal(age),
112:    itsBreed(breed)
113:    {
114:        cout << "Dog(int, BREED) constructor...\n";
115:    }
116:
117:    Dog::~Dog()
118:    {
119:        cout << "Dog destructor...\n";
120:    }
121:    int main()
122:    {
123:        Dog fido;
124:        Dog rover(5);
125:        Dog buster(6,8);
126:        Dog yorkie (3,YORKIE);
127:        Dog dobbie (4,20,DOBERMAN);
128:        fido.Speak();
129:        rover.WagTail();
130:        cout << "Yorkie is " << yorkie.GetAge();
131:        cout << " years old\n";
132:        cout << "Dobbie weighs " << dobbie.GetWeight();
133:        cout << " pounds\n";
134:      return 0;
135:    }
```

Line Numbers in Output   The output has been numbered so each line can be referred to in the analysis. These numbers do not print in the actual output.

OUTPUT

```
1:  Mammal constructor...
2:  Dog constructor...
3:  Mammal(int) constructor...
4:  Dog(int) constructor...
5:  Mammal(int) constructor...
6:  Dog(int, int) constructor...
7:  Mammal(int) constructor...
8:  Dog(int, BREED) constructor....
9:  Mammal(int) constructor...
10: Dog(int, int, BREED) constructor...
11: Mammal sound!
12: Tail wagging...
13: Yorkie is 3 years old.
14: Dobie weighs 20 pounds.
15: Dog destructor. . .
16: Mammal destructor...
17: Dog destructor...
18: Mammal destructor...
19: Dog destructor...
20: Mammal destructor...
21: Dog destructor...
22: Mammal destructor...
23: Dog destructor...
24: Mammal destructor...
```

In Listing 22.1, Mammal's constructor has been overloaded on line 14 to take an integer, the Mammal's age. The implementation on lines 68–73 initializes itsAge with the value passed into the constructor, and itsWeight with the value 5.

Dog has overloaded five constructors, on lines 40–44. The first is the default constructor. The second takes the age, which is the same parameter the Mammal constructor takes. The third constructor takes both the age and the weight, the fourth takes the age and breed, and the fifth takes the age, weight, and breed.

Note that on line 81 Dog's default constructor calls Mammal's default constructor. Although it is not strictly necessary to do this, it serves as documentation that you intended to call the base constructor, which takes no parameters. The base constructor would be called in any case, but actually doing so makes your intentions explicit.

The implementation for the Dog constructor, which takes an integer, is on lines 87–92. In its initialization phase (lines 88–89), Dog initializes its base class, passing in the parameter, and then it initializes its breed.

Another Dog constructor is on lines 94–100. This one takes two parameters. Once again it initializes its base class by calling the appropriate constructor, but this time it also assigns weight to its base class's variable itsWeight. Note that you cannot assign to the base class variable in the initialization phase. Because Mammal does not have a constructor that takes this parameter, you must do this within the body of the Dog's constructor.

Walk through the remaining constructors to make sure you are comfortable with how they work. Note what is initialized and what must wait for the body of the constructor.

The output has been numbered so that each line can be referred to in this analysis. The first two lines of output represent the instantiation of Fido, using the default constructor.

In the output, lines 3 and 4 represent the creation of rover. Lines 5 and 6 represent buster. Note that the Mammal constructor that was called is the constructor that takes one integer, but the Dog constructor is the constructor that takes two integers.

After all the objects are created, they are used and then go out of scope. As each object is destroyed, first the Dog destructor and then the Mammal destructor is called; there are five of each in total.

OVERRIDING FUNCTIONS

A Dog object has access to all the member functions in class Mammal, as well as to any member functions, such as WagTail(), that the declaration of the Dog class might add. It can also override a base class function. Overriding a function means changing the implementation of a base class function in a derived class. When you make an object of the derived class, the correct function is called.

When a derived class creates a function with the same return type and signature as a member function in the base class, but with a new implementation, it is said to be *overriding* that method.

When you override a function, it must agree in return type and in signature with the function in the base class. The signature is the function prototype other than the return type: that is, the name, the parameter list, and the keyword const, if used.

The signature of a function is its name, as well as the number, and type of its parameters. The signature does not include the return type.

Listing 22.2 illustrates what happens if the Dog class overrides the speak() method in Mammal. To save room, the accessor functions have been left out of these classes.

LISTING 22.2   OVERRIDING A BASE CLASS METHOD IN A DERIVED CLASS

```
1:      //Listing 22.2 Overriding a base class method
2:
3:      #include <iostream.h>
4:      enum BREED
5:      {
6:          YORKIE, CAIRN, DANDIE, SHETLAND, DOBERMAN, LAB
7:      };
8:
9:      class Mammal
10:     {
11:     public:
12:         // constructors
13:         Mammal() { cout << "Mammal constructor...\n"; }
14:         ~Mammal() { cout << "Mammal destructor...\n"; }
15:
16:         //Other methods
17:         void Speak()const { cout << "Mammal sound!\n"; }
18:         void Sleep()const
19:             { cout << "shhh. I'm sleeping.\n"; }
20:
21:
22:     protected:
23:         int itsAge;
24:         int itsWeight;
25:     };
26:
```

continues

LISTING 22.2   CONTINUED

```
27:     class Dog : public Mammal
28:     {
29:     public:
30:
31:         // Constructors
32:         Dog(){ cout << "Dog constructor...\n"; }
33:         ~Dog(){ cout << "Dog destructor...\n"; }
34:
35:         // Other methods
36:         void WagTail() const { cout << "Tail wagging...\n"; }
37:         void BegForFood() const
38:             { cout << "Begging for food...\n"; }
39:         void Speak() const { cout << "Woof!\n"; }
40:
41:     private:
42:         BREED itsBreed;
43:     };
44:
45:     int main()
46:     {
47:         Mammal bigAnimal;
48:         Dog fido;
49:         bigAnimal.Speak();
50:         fido.Speak();
51:       return 0;
52:     }
```

OUTPUT

```
Mammal constructor...
Mammal constructor...
Dog constructor...
Mammal sound!
Woof!
Dog destructor...
Mammal destructor...
Mammal destructor...
```

On line 39, the Dog class overrides the Speak() method, causing Dog objects to say Woof! when the Speak() method is called. On line 47, a Mammal object, bigAnimal, is created, causing the first line of output when the Mammal constructor is called. On line 48, a Dog object, fido, is created, causing the next two lines of output, where the Mammal constructor and then the Dog constructor are called.

On line 49, the Mammal object calls its Speak() method; then on line 50, the Dog object calls its Speak() method. The output reflects that the correct methods were called. Finally, the two objects go out of scope and the destructors are called.

OVERLOADING VERSUS OVERRIDING

These terms are similar and they do similar things. When you overload a method you create more than one method with the same name, but with a different signature. When you override a method, you create a method in a derived class with the same name as a method in the base class and the same signature.

HIDING THE BASE CLASS METHOD

In the previous listing, the Dog class's method Speak() hides the base class's method. This is just what is wanted, but it can have unexpected results. If Mammal has a method, Move() that is overloaded, and Dog overrides that method, the Dog method will hide all the Mammal methods with that name.

If Mammal overloads Move() as three methods—one that takes no parameters, one that takes an integer, and one that takes an integer and a direction—and Dog overrides just the Move() method, which takes no parameters, it will not be easy to access the other two methods using a Dog object.

CALLING THE BASE METHOD

If you have overridden the base method, it is still possible to call it by fully qualifying the name of the method. You do this by writing the base name, followed by two colons and then the method name. Listing 22.3 illustrates how to do this

```
Mammal::Move()
```

LISTING 22.3   CALLING THE BASE METHOD

```
1:    //Listing 22.3 Calling base method from overridden
      ➥method.
2:
3:    #include <iostream.h>
4:
5:    class Mammal
6:    {
7:    public:
8:        void Move() const
9:           { cout << "Mammal move one step\n"; }
10:        void Move(int distance) const
11:        {
12:            cout << "Mammal move ";
13:            cout << distance << " steps.\n";
14:        }
15:    protected:
16:        int itsAge;
17:        int itsWeight;
18:    };
19:
20:    class Dog : public Mammal
21:    {
22:    public:
23:        void Move()const;
24:    };
25:
26:    void Dog::Move() const
27:    {
28:        cout << "In dog move...\n";
29:        Mammal::Move(3);
30:    }
31:
32:    int main()
33:    {
34:        Mammal bigAnimal;
35:        Dog fido;
36:        bigAnimal.Move(2);
37:        fido.Mammal::Move(6);
38:    return 0;
39:    }
```

OUTPUT

```
Mammal move 2    _steps
Mammal move 6    _steps
```

On line 34, a `Mammal`, `bigAnimal`, is created, and on line 35, a `Dog`, `Fido`, is created. The method call on line 36 invokes the `Move()` method of `Mammal`, which takes an `int`.

The programmer wanted to invoke `Move(int)` on the `Dog` object, but had a problem. `Dog` overrides the `Move()` method, but does not overload it and does not provide a version that takes an `int`. This is solved by the explicit call to the base class `Move(int)` method on line 37.

In this lesson, you learned how to call the constructor in base objects and how to override implementation in derived objects.

LESSON 23

POLYMORPHISM

In this lesson, you will learn how virtual methods enable you to use your base classes polymorphically.

VIRTUAL METHODS

In the previous lesson, "Issues in Inheritance," you learned about inheritance and how derived classes can create an inheritance hierarchy. You also saw how methods in the base class can be overridden in the derived class.

It emphasized the fact that a Dog object is a Mammal object. So far that has meant only that the Dog object has inherited the attributes (data) and capabilities (methods) of its base class. In C++, the *is-a* relationship runs deeper than that, however.

C++ extends its polymorphism to enable pointers to base classes to be assigned to derived class objects. Therefore, you can write

```
Mammal* pMammal = new Dog;
```

This creates a new Dog object on the heap and returns a pointer to that object, which it assigns to a pointer to Mammal. This is fine, because a Dog is a Mammal.

You can then use this pointer to invoke any method on Mammal. You want those methods that are overridden in Dog to call the correct function. Virtual member functions let you do that. Listing 23.1 illustrates how this works, and what happens with non-virtual methods.

Assigning object addresses This ability to assign the address of an object of a derived class to a pointer to a base class is the essence of polymorphism. You could, for example, create many different types of windows—including dialog boxes, scrollable windows, and list boxes—and give them each a virtual draw() method. By creating a pointer to window and assigning dialog boxes and other derived types to that pointer, you can call draw() without regard to the actual runtime type of the object pointed to. The correct draw() function will be called.

LISTING 23.1 USING VIRTUAL METHODS

```
1:      //Listing 17.123.1 Using virtual methods
2:
3:      #include <iostream.h>
4:
5:      class Mammal
6:      {
7:      public:
8:              Mammal():itsAge(1)
9:              {
10:                     cout << ""Mammal constructor...\n"";
11:             }
12:             virtual ~Mammal()
13:             {
14:                     cout << ""Mammal destructor...\n"";
15:             }
16:             void Move() const
17:             {
18:                     cout << ""Mammal move one step\n"";
19:             }
20:             virtual void Speak() const
21:             {
22:                     cout << ""Mammal speak!\n"";
23:             }
24:      protected:
25:             int itsAge;
26:
```

continues

LISTING 23.1   CONTINUED

```
27:      };
28:
29:      class Dog : public Mammal
30:      {
31:      public:
32:              Dog()
33:              {
34:                      cout << ""Dog constructor...\n"";
35:              }
36:              ~Dog()
37:              {
38:                      cout << ""Dog destructor...\n"";
39:              }
40:              void WagTail() const
41:              {
42:                      cout << ""Wagging Tail...\n"";
43:              }
44:              void Speak()const
45:              {
46:                      cout << ""Woof!\n"";
47:              }
48:              void Move()const
49:              {
50:                      cout << ""Dog moves 5 steps...\n"";
51:              }
52:      };
53:
54:      int main()
55:      {
56:
57:              Mammal *pDog = new Dog;
58:              pDog->Move();
59:              pDog->Speak();
60:
61:              return 0;
62:      }
```

OUTPUT

```
Mammal constructor...
Dog Constructor...
Mammal move one step
Woof!
```

On line 20, Mammal is provided a virtual method—speak(). The designer of this class thereby signals that she expects this class to eventually be another class's base type. The derived class will probably want to override this function.

On line 57, a pointer to Mammal is created, pDog, but it is assigned the address of a new Dog object. Because a Dog is a Mammal, this is a legal assignment. The pointer is then used to call the Move() function. Because the compiler knows pDog only to be a Mammal, it looks to the Mammal object to find the Move() method.

On line 59, the pointer then calls the Speak() method. Because Speak() is virtual, the Speak() method overridden in Dog is invoked.

This is almost magical. As far as the calling function knows, it has a Mammal pointer; but here a method on Dog is called. In fact, if you had an array of pointers to Mammal, each of which pointed to a subclass of Mammal, you could call each in turn and the correct function would be called.

HOW VIRTUAL MEMBER FUNCTIONS WORK

When a derived object, such as a Dog object, is created, first the constructor for the base class is called and then the constructor for the derived class is called. Figure 23.1 shows what the Dog object looks like after it is created. Note that the Mammal part of the object is contiguous in memory with the Dog part.

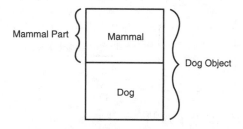

FIGURE 23.1   The Dog object after it is created.

When a virtual function is created in an object, the object must keep track of that function. Many compilers build a virtual function table, called a *v-table*. One of these is kept for each type, and each object of that type keeps a virtual table pointer (called a vptr or *v-pointer*), which points to that table.

Although implementations vary, all compilers must accomplish the same thing; so you won't be too wrong with this description.

Each object's vptr points to the v-table that, in turn, has a pointer to each of the virtual member functions. When the Mammal part of the Dog is created, the vptr is initialized to point to the correct part of the v-table, as shown in Figure 23.2.

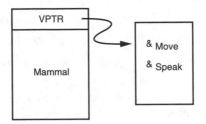

FIGURE 23.2   The v-table of a Mammal.

When the Dog constructor is called and the Dog part of this object is added, the vptr is adjusted to point to the virtual function overrides (if any) in the Dog object, as illustrated in Figure 23.3.

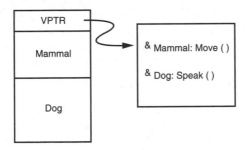

FIGURE 23.3   The v-table of a Dog.

When a pointer to a Mammal is used, the vptr continues to point to the correct function, depending on the real type of the object. Thus, when Speak() is invoked, the correct function is invoked.

YOU CAN'T GET THERE FROM HERE

If the Dog object had a method, WagTail(), that was not in the Mammal, you could not use the pointer to Mammal to access that method (unless you cast it to be a pointer to Dog). Because WagTail() is not a virtual function, and because it is not in a `Mammal` object, you can't get there without either a `Dog` object or a `Dog` pointer.

Although you can transform the `Mammal` pointer into a `Dog` pointer, there are usually far better and safer ways to call the `WagTail()` method. We'll see this later in the book.

 Using Virtual Functions   Virtual function magic only operates on pointers and references. Passing an object by value will not enable the virtual member functions to be invoked.

VIRTUAL DESTRUCTORS

It is legal and common to pass a pointer to a derived object when a pointer to a base object is expected. What happens when that pointer to a derived subject is deleted? If the destructor is virtual, as it should be, the right thing happens—the derived class's destructor is called. Because the derived class's destructor will automatically invoke the base class's destructor, the entire object will be properly destroyed.

The rule of thumb is this: If any of the functions in your class are virtual, the destructor should be as well.

THE COST OF VIRTUAL METHODS

Because objects with virtual methods must maintain a v-table, there is some overhead in having virtual methods. If you have a very small class from which you do not expect to derive other classes, there might be no reason to have any virtual methods.

Once you declare any methods virtual, you've paid most of the price of the v-table (although each entry does add a small memory overhead). At that point, you'll want the destructor to be virtual, and the assumption is that all other methods probably are virtual as well. Take a long, hard look at any non-virtual methods, and be certain you understand why they are not virtual.

In this lesson, you learned how virtual methods can be used to create polymorphism.

LESSON 24

ADVANCED POLYMORPHISM

In this lesson, you will learn about abstract data types and pure virtual functions.

ABSTRACT DATA TYPES

Often, you will create a hierarchy of classes together. For example, you might create a Shape class, and derive from it Rectangle and Circle. From Rectangle, you might derive Square as a special case of Rectangle.

Each of the derived classes will override the Draw() method, the GetArea() method, and so forth. Listing 24.1 illustrates a bare-bones implementation of the Shape class and its derived Circle and Rectangle classes.

LISTING 24.1 Shape CLASSES

```
1:      //Listing 24.1. Shape classes.
2:
3:      #include <iostream.h>
4:
5:
6:
7:      class Shape
8:      {
9:      public:
10:        Shape(){}
11:        virtual ~Shape(){}
12:        virtual long GetArea() const { return -1; }
13:        virtual long GetPerim() const { return -1; }
14:        virtual void Draw() const {}
15:      private:
16:      };
17:
18:      class Circle : public Shape
19:      {
```

```
20:     public:
21:            Circle(int radius):itsRadius(radius){}
22:            ~Circle(){}
23:            long GetArea() const
24:                { return 3 * itsRadius * itsRadius; }
25:            long GetPerim() const { return 9 * itsRadius; }
26:            void Draw() const;
27:     private:
28:         int itsRadius;
29:         int itsCircumference;
30:     };
31:
32:     void Circle::Draw() const
33:     {
34:         cout << "Circle drawing routine here!\n";
35:     }
36:
37:
38:     class Rectangle : public Shape
39:     {
40:     public:
41:            Rectangle(int len, int width):
42:                itsLength(len), itsWidth(width){}
43:            virtual ~Rectangle(){}
44:            virtual long GetArea() const
45:                { return itsLength * itsWidth; }
46:            virtual long GetPerim() const
                ➥{return 2*itsLength + 2*itsWidth; }
47:            virtual int GetLength() const
48:                { return itsLength; }
49:            virtual int GetWidth() const
                ➥{ return itsWidth; }
50:            virtual void Draw() const;
51:     private:
52:         int itsWidth;
53:         int itsLength;
54:     };
55:
56:     void Rectangle::Draw() const
57:     {
58:         for (int i = 0; i<itsLength; i++)
59:         {
60:             for (int j = 0; j<itsWidth; j++)
61:                 cout << "x ";
62:
63:             cout << "\n";
64:         }
```

continues

LISTING 24.1   CONTINUED

```
65:     }
66:
67:     class Square : public Rectangle
68:     {
69:     public:
70:             Square(int len);
71:             Square(int len, int width);
72:             ~Square(){}
73:             long GetPerim() const {return 4 * GetLength();}
74:     };
75:
76:     Square::Square(int len):
77:         Rectangle(len,len)
78:     {}
79:
80:     Square::Square(int len, int width):
81:         Rectangle(len,width)
82:
83:     {
84:         if (GetLength() != GetWidth())
85:         {
86:             cout << "Error, not a square... ";
87:             cout << " a Rectangle??\n";
88:         }
89:     }
90:
91:     int main()
92:     {
93:         int choice;
94:         bool fQuit = false;
95:         Shape * sp;
96:
97:         while (1)
98:         {
99:             cout << "(1)Circle (2)Rectangle ";
                 cout << " (3)Square (0)Quit: ";
100:            cin >> choice;
101:
102:            switch (choice)
103:            {
104:                case 1: sp = new Circle(5);
105:                 break;
106:                case 2: sp = new Rectangle(4,6);
107:                break;
108:                case 3: sp = new Square(5);
109:                break;
```

```
110:                default: fQuit = true;
111:                break;
112:            }
113:            if (fQuit)
114:                break;
115:
116:            sp->Draw();
117:            cout << "\n";
118:        }
119:     return 0;
120:    }
```

```
 (1)Circle (2)Rectangle (3)Square (0)Quit: 2
x x x x x x
x x x x x x
x x x x x x
x x x x x x
 (1)Circle (2)Rectangle (3)Square (0)Quit:3
x x x x x
x x x x x
x x x x x
x x x x x
x x x x x
 (1)Circle (2)Rectangle (3)Square (0)Quit:0
```

On lines 7–16, the Shape class is declared. The GetArea() and GetPerim() methods return an error value, and Draw() takes no action. After all, what does it mean to draw a shape? Only types of shapes (circles, rectangle, and so on) can be drawn; shapes as an abstraction cannot be drawn.

Circle derives from Shape and overrides the three virtual methods. Note that there is no reason to add the word virtual, as that is part of their inheritance. But there is no harm in doing so either, as shown in the Rectangle class on lines 43–50. It is a good idea to include the term virtual as a reminder, a form of documentation.

Square derives from Rectangle, and it too overrides the GetPerim() method, inheriting the rest of the methods defined in Rectangle.

It is troubling, though, that a client might try to instantiate a Shape object, and it might be desirable to make that impossible. The Shape class exists only to provide an interface for the classes derived from it; as such, it is an abstract data type, or ADT.

An abstract data type represents a concept (like shape) rather than an object (like circle). In C++, an ADT is always the base class to other classes, and it is not valid to make an instance of an ADT.

PURE VIRTUAL FUNCTIONS

C++ supports the creation of abstract data types with pure virtual functions. A virtual function is made pure by initializing it with 0, as in:

```
virtual void Draw() = 0;
```

Any class with one or more pure virtual functions is an ADT, and it is illegal to instantiate an object of a class that is an ADT. Trying to do so will cause a compile-time error. Putting a pure virtual function in your class signals two things to clients of your class:

- Don't make an object of this class derive from it.

- Make sure you override the pure virtual function.

Any class that derives from an ADT inherits the pure virtual function as pure, and so must override every pure virtual function if it wants to instantiate objects. Therefore, if Rectangle inherits from Shape, and Shape has three pure virtual functions, Rectangle must override all three or it too will be an ADT. Listing 24.2 rewrites the Shape class to be an abstract data type. To save space, the rest of Listing 24.1 is not reproduced here. Replace the declaration of Shape in Listing 24.1, lines 7–16, with the declaration of Shape in Listing 24.2 and run the program again.

LISTING 24.2   ABSTRACT DATA TYPES

```
1:   class Shape
2:   {
3:   public:
4:         Shape(){}
5:         virtual ~Shape(){}
6:         virtual long GetArea() const = 0;
7:         virtual long GetPerim() const = 0;
8:         virtual void Draw() const = 0;
9:   private:
10: };
```

```
(1)Circle (2)Rectangle (3)Square (0)Quit:2
x x x x x x
x x x x x x
x x x x x x
x x x x x x
 (1)Circle (2)Rectangle (3)Square (0)Quit:3
x x x x x
x x x x x
x x x x x
x x x x x
x x x x x
 (1)Circle (2)Rectangle (3)Square (0)Quit:0
```

As you can see, the workings of the program are totally unaffected. The only difference is that it would now be impossible to make an object of class Shape.

 Abstract Data Types   You declare a class to be an abstract data type by including one or more pure virtual functions in the class declaration. Declare a pure virtual function by writing = 0 after the function declaration. For example

```
class Shape
{
virtual void Draw() = 0;    // pure virtual
};
```

IMPLEMENTING PURE VIRTUAL FUNCTIONS

Typically, the pure virtual functions in an abstract base class are never implemented. Because no objects of that type are ever created, there is no reason to provide implementations, and the ADT works purely as the definition of an interface to objects that derive from it.

It is possible, however, to provide an implementation to a pure virtual function. The function can then be called by objects derived from the ADT, perhaps to provide common functionality to all the overridden functions.

COMPLEX HIERARCHIES OF ABSTRACTION

At times, you will derive ADTs from other ADTs. It might be that you will want to make some of the derived pure virtual functions non-pure, and leave others pure.

If you create the `Animal` class, you can make `Eat()`, `Sleep()`, `Move()`, and `Reproduce()` be pure virtual functions. Perhaps from `Animal` you would derive `Mammal` and `Fish`.

On examination, you decide that every `Mammal` will reproduce in the same way, and so you make `Mammal::Reproduce()` be non-pure, but you leave `Eat()`, `Sleep()`, and `Move()` as pure virtual functions.

From `Mammal` you derive `Dog`, and `Dog` must override and implement the three remaining pure virtual functions so that you can make objects of type `Dog`.

What you've said, as class designer, is that no `Animal`s or `Mammal`s can be instantiated, but that all `Mammal`s might inherit the provided `Reproduce()` method without overriding it.

WHICH TYPES ARE ABSTRACT?

In one program, the class `Animal` is abstract; in another, it is not. What determines whether to make a class abstract?

The answer to this question is decided not by any real-world intrinsic factor, but by what makes sense in your program. If you are writing a program that depicts a farm or a zoo, you might want `Animal` to be an abstract data type, but `Dog` to be a class from which you can instantiate objects.

On the other hand, if you are making an animated kennel, you might want to keep `Dog` as an abstract data type, and only instantiate types of dogs: retrievers, terriers, and so forth. The level of abstraction is a function of how finely you need to distinguish your types.

In this lesson, you learned what abstract data types are and how to create them.

LESSON 25
LINKED LISTS

In this lesson, you will focus on one type of structure, a linked list, that can be used to create collections of objects.

LINKED LISTS AND OTHER STRUCTURES

Advanced programming requires the creation of complex structures, often called *collections*, that are used to store and manipulate objects.

Arrays are much like Tupperware. They are great containers, but they are of a fixed size. If you pick a container that is too large, you waste space in your storage area. If you pick one that is too small, its contents spill all over and you have a big mess.

One way to solve this problem is with a linked list. A *linked list* is a data structure or collection consisting of small containers that "snap together." The idea is to write a class that holds one object of your data—such as one CAT or one Rectangle—and that also points at the next container in the list. You create one container for each object that you need to store, and you chain them together as needed.

The containers are called *nodes*. The first node in the list is called the *head*, and the last node in the list is called the *tail*.

Lists come in three fundamental forms. From simplest to most complex, they are

> Singly linked
>
> Doubly linked
>
> Trees

In a *singly linked list*, each node points to the next one, but not backward. To find a particular node, you start at the top and go from node to node, as in a treasure hunt. ("The next node is under the sofa.") A *doubly linked list* enables you move backward and forward in the chain. A *tree* is a complex structure built from nodes. Each node can point in two or three directions. Figure 25.1 shows these three fundamental structures.

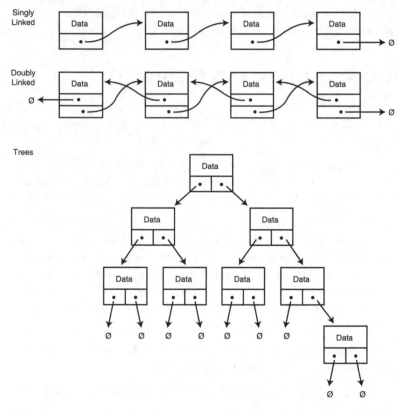

FIGURE 25.1   Linked lists.

Computer scientists have created even more complex and clever data structures, nearly all of which rely on interconnecting nodes.

A CASE STUDY

In this lesson, we will examine a linked list in detail, as a case study both of how you create complex structures and, more important, how you use inheritance, polymorphism, and encapsulation to manage large projects.

DELEGATION OF RESPONSIBILITY

A fundamental premise of object-oriented programming is that each object does one thing very well, and delegates to other objects anything that is not its core mission.

An automobile is a perfect example of this idea in hardware: the engine's job is to produce the power. Distribution of that power is not the engine's job; that is up to the transmission. Turning is not the job of the engine nor the transmission; that is delegated to the wheels.

A well-designed machine has lots of small, well-understood parts, each doing its own job and working together to accomplish a greater good. A well-designed program is much the same: each class sticks to its own knitting, but together they create a heck of an afghan.

THE COMPONENT PARTS

The linked list will consist of nodes. The node class itself will be abstract; we'll use three subtypes to accomplish the work. There will be a head node whose job is to manage the head of the list, a tail node (guess what its job is!), and zero or more internal nodes. The internal nodes will keep track of the actual data to be held in the list.

Note that the data and the list are quite distinct. You can, in theory, save any type of data you like in a list. It isn't the data that is linked together; it is the nodes that *hold* the data.

The driver program doesn't know about the nodes; it works with the list. The list, however, does little work; it simply delegates to the nodes.

Listing 25.1 shows the code; we'll examine it in excruciating detail.

LISTING 25.1   A LINKED LIST

```
0:      // **************************************************
1:      //      FILE:           Listing 25.1
2:      //
3:      //      PURPOSE:        Demonstrate ilinked list
4:      //      NOTES:
5:      //
6:      //
7:      //                      All Rights Reserved
8:      //
9:      // Demonstrates an object-oriented approach to
10:     // linked lists. The list delegates to the node.
11:     // The node is an abstract data type. Three types of
12:     // nodes are used, headnodes, tailnodes and internal
13:     // nodes. Only the internal nodes hold data.
14:   //
15:   // The Data class is created to serve as an object to
16:     // hold in the linked list.
17:     //
18:     // **************************************************
19:
20:
21:     #include <iostream.h>
22:
23:     enum { kIsSmaller, kIsLarger, kIsSame};
24:
25:     // Data class to put into the linked list
26:     // Any class in this linked list must support two
      ➥methods:
27:     // Show (displays the value) and Compare28:     class
      ➥Data
29:     {
30:     public:
31:         Data(int val):myValue(val){}
32:         ~Data(){}
33:         int Compare(const Data &) const;
34:         void Show() const { cout << myValue << endl; }
35:     private:
36:         int myValue;
37:     };
38:
39:     // Compare is used to decide where in the list
40:     // a particular object belongs.
41:     int Data::Compare(const Data & theOtherData) const
42:     {
43:         if (myValue < theOtherData.myValue)
44:             return kIsSmaller;
```

```
45:              if (myValue > theOtherData.myValue)
46:                  return kIsLarger;
47:              else
48:                  return kIsSame;
49:      }
50:
51:      // forward declarations
52:      class Node;
53:      class HeadNode;
54:      class TailNode;
55:      class InternalNode;
56:
57:      // ADT representing the node object in the list
58:      // Every derived class must override Insert and Show
59:      class Node
60:      {
61:      public:
62:          Node(){}
63:          virtual ~Node(){}
64:          virtual Node * Insert(Data * theData)=0;
65:          virtual void Show() const = 0;
66:      private:
67:      };
68:
69:      // This is the node which holds the actual object
70:      // In this case the object is of type Data
71:      // We'll see how to make this more general when
72:      // we cover templates
73:      class InternalNode: public Node
74:      {
75:      public:
76:          InternalNode(Data * theData, Node * next);
77:          virtual ~InternalNode()
77a:             { delete myNext; delete myData; }
78:          virtual Node * Insert(Data * theData);
79:          virtual void Show() const
79a:             { myData->Show(); myNext->Show(); }  80:
81:      private:
82:              Data * myData;  // the data itself
83:              Node * myNext; 84:     };
85:
86:      // All the constructor does is to initialize
87:      InternalNode::InternalNode
87a:         (Data * theData, Node * next):
88:      myData(theData),myNext(next)
89:      {
90:      }
```

continues

LISTING 25.1   CONTINUED

```
91:
92:     // the meat of the list
93:     // When you put a new object into the list
94:     // it is passed ot the node which figures out
95:     // where it goes and inserts it into the list
96:     Node * InternalNode::Insert(Data * theData)
97:     {
98:
99:         // is the new guy bigger or smaller than me?
100:        int result = myData->Compare(*theData);
101:
102:
103:        switch(result)
104:        {
105:    // by convention if it is the same it comes first
106:        case kIsSame:        // fall through
107:        case kIsLarger:      // new data comes before me
108:            {
109:                InternalNode * dataNode =
109a:                   new InternalNode(theData, this);
110:                return dataNode;
111:            }
112:
113:            // bigger than I am so pass it on to the
114:            // next node and let HIM handle it.
115:        case kIsSmaller:
116:                myNext = myNext->Insert(theData);
117:                return this;
118:        }
119:        return this;   // appease MSC
120:    }
121:
122:
123:    // Tail node is just a sentinel
124:
125:    class TailNode : public Node
126:    {
127:    public:
128:        TailNode(){}
129:        virtual ~TailNode(){}
130:        virtual Node * Insert(Data * theData);
131:        virtual void Show() const { }
132:
133:    private:
134:
```

```
135:      };
136:
137:      // must be inserted before me
138:      // as I am the tail and NOTHING comes after me
139:      Node * TailNode::Insert(Data * theData)
140:      {
141:          InternalNode * dataNode =
141a:             new InternalNode(theData, this);
142:          return dataNode;
143:      }
144:
145:      // Head node has no data, it just points
146:      // to the very beginning of the list
147:      class HeadNode : public Node
148:      {
149:      public:
150:          HeadNode();
151:          virtual ~HeadNode() { delete myNext; }
152:          virtual Node * Insert(Data * theData);
153:          virtual void Show() const { myNext->Show(); }
154:      private:
155:          Node * myNext;
156:      };
157:
158:      // As soon as the head is created
159:      // it creates the tail
160:      HeadNode::HeadNode()
161:      {
162:          myNext = new TailNode;
163:      }
164:
165:      // Nothing comes before the head so just
166:      // pass the data on to the next node
167:      Node * HeadNode::Insert(Data * theData)
168:      {
169:          myNext = myNext->Insert(theData);
170:          return this;
171:      }
172:
173:      // I get all the credit and do none of the work
174:      class LinkedList
175:      {
176:      public:
177:          LinkedList();
178:          ~LinkedList() { delete myHead; }
179:          void Insert(Data * theData);
```

continues

LISTING 25.1   CONTINUED

```
180:          void ShowAll() const { myHead->Show(); }
181:      private:
182:          HeadNode * myHead;
183:      };
184:
185:      // At birth, i create the head node
186:      // It creates the tail node
187:      // So an empty list points to the head which
188:      // points to the tail and has nothing between
189:      LinkedList::LinkedList()
190:      {
191:          myHead = new HeadNode;
192:      }
193:
194:      // Delegate, delegate, delegate
195:      void LinkedList::Insert(Data * pData)
196:      {
197:          myHead->Insert(pData);
198:      }
199:
200:      // test driver program
201:      int main()
202:      {
203:          Data * pData;
204:          int val;
205:          LinkedList ll;
206:
207:          // ask the user to produce some values
208:          // put them in the list
209:          for (;;)
210:          {
211:              cout << "What value? (0 to stop): ";
212:              cin >> val;
213:              if (!val)
214:                  break;
215:              pData = new Data(val);
216:              ll.Insert(pData);
217:          }
218:
219:          // now walk the list and show the data
220:          ll.ShowAll();
221:          return 0;
222:      }
```

```
What value? (0 to stop): 5
What value? (0 to stop): 8
What value? (0 to stop): 3
What value? (0 to stop): 9
What value? (0 to stop): 2
What value? (0 to stop): 10
What value? (0 to stop): 0
2
3
5
8
9
10
```

The first thing to note is the enumerated constant, which provides three constant values: `kIsSmaller`, `kIsLarger`, and `kIsSame`. Every object that may be held in this linked list must support a `Compare()` method. These constants will be the result value returned by the `Compare()` method.

For illustration purposes, the class `Data` is created on lines 28–37, and the `Compare()` method is implemented on lines 39–49. A `Data` object holds a value and can compare itself with other `Data` objects. It also supports a `Show()` method to display the value of the `Data` object.

The easiest way to understand the workings of the linked list is to step through an example of using one. On line 201, a driver program is declared; on line 203, a pointer to a `Data` object is declared; and on line 205, a local linked list is defined.

When the linked list is created, the constructor on line 189 is called. The only work done in the constructor is to allocate a `HeadNode` object and to assign that object's address to the pointer held in the linked list on line 182.

This allocation of a `HeadNode` invokes the `HeadNode` constructor shown on line 160. This in turn allocates a `TailNode` and assigns its address to the `HeadNode`'s `myNext` pointer. The creation of the `TailNode` calls the `TailNode` constructor shown on line 128, which is inline and which does nothing.

Thus, by the simple act of allocating a linked list on the stack, the list is created, a head and a tail node are created, and their relationship is established, as illustrated in Figure 25.2.

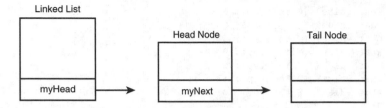

FIGURE 25.2   The linked list after it is created.

Line 209 begins an infinite loop. The user will be prompted for values to add to the linked list. He can add as many values as he likes, entering 0 when he is finished. The code on line 213 evaluates the value entered; if it is 0, it breaks out of the loop.

If the value is not 0, a new Data object is created on line 215, and that is inserted into the list on line 216. For illustration purposes, assume the user enters the value 15. This invokes the Insert method on line 195.

The linked list immediately delegates responsibility for inserting the object to its head node. This invokes the method Insert on line 167. The head node immediately passes the responsibility to whatever node its myNext is pointing to. In this (first) case, it is pointing to the tail node (remember, when the head node was born it created a link to a tail node). This, therefore, invokes the method Insert on line 139.

TailNode::Insert knows that the object it has been handed must be inserted immediately before itself—that is, the new object will be in the list right before the tail node. Therefore, on line 141, it creates a new InternalNode object, passing in the data and a pointer to itself. This invokes the constructor for the InternalNode object, shown on line 87.

The InternalNode constructor does nothing more than initialize its Data pointer with the address of the Data object it was passed and its myNext pointer with the node's address it was passed. In this case, the node it will point to is the tail node (remember, the tail node passed in its own this pointer).

Now that the InternalNode has been created, the address of that internal node is assigned to the pointer dataNode on line 141, and that address is in turn returned from the TailNode::Insert() method. This returns us to HeadNode::Insert(), where the address of the InternalNode is assigned to the HeadNode's myNext pointer (on line 169). Finally, the HeadNode's address is returned to the linked list where, on line 197, it is thrown away. (Nothing is done with it because the linked list already knows the address of the HeadNode.)

Why bother returning the address if it is not used? Insert is declared in the base class, Node. The return value is needed by the other implementations. If you change the return value of HeadNode::Insert(), you will get a compiler error; it is simpler just to return the HeadNode and let the linked list throw its address on the floor.

So what happened? The data was inserted into the list. The list passed it to the head. The head blindly passed the data to whatever the head happened to be pointing to. In this (first) case, the head was pointing to the tail. The tail immediately created a new internal node, initializing the new node to point to the tail. The tail then returned the address of the new node to the head, which reassigned its myNext pointer to point to the new node. Hey! Presto! The data is in the list in the right place, as illustrated in Figure 25.3.

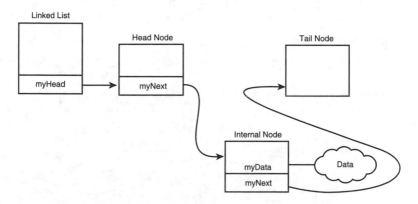

FIGURE 25.3   The linked list after the first node is inserted.

After inserting the first node, program control resumes at line 211. Once again the value is evaluated. For illustration purposes, assume that the value 3 is entered. This causes a new Data object to be created on line 215 and to be inserted into the list on line 216.

Once again, on line 197 the list passes the data to its HeadNode. The HeadNode::Insert() method in turn passes the new value to whatever its myNext happens to be pointing to. As you know, it is now pointing to the node that contains the Data object whose value is 15. This invokes the InternalNode::Insert() method on line 96.

On line 100, the InternalNode uses its myData pointer to tell its Data object (the one whose value is 15) to call its Compare() method, passing in the new Data object (whose value is 3). This invokes the Compare() method shown on line 41.

The two values are compared; and, because myValue will be 15 and theOtherData.myValue will be 3, the returned value will be kIsLarger. This will cause program flow to jump to line 109.

A new InternalNode is created for the new Data object. The new node will point to the current InternalNode object, and the new InternalNode's address is returned from the InternalNode::Insert() method to the HeadNode. Thus, the new node, whose object's value is smaller than the current node's object's value, is inserted into the list, and the list now looks like Figure 25.4.

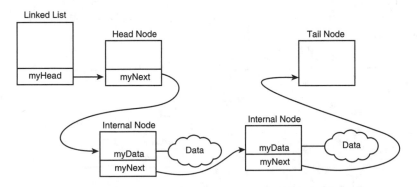

FIGURE 25.4   The linked list after the second node is inserted.

In the third invocation of the loop, the customer adds the value 8. This is larger than 3 but smaller than 15, and so should be inserted between the two existing nodes. Progress will be exactly like the previous example, except that when the node whose object's value is 3 does the compare, rather than returning `kIsLarger`, it will return `kIsSmaller` (meaning that the object whose value is 3 is smaller than the new object, whose value is 8).

This will cause the `InternalNode::Insert()` method to branch to line 116. Rather than creating a new node and inserting it, the `InternalNode` will just pass the new data on to the `Insert` method of whatever its `myNext` pointer happens to be pointing to. In this case, it will invoke `InsertNode` on the `InternalNode` whose `Data` object's value is 15.

The comparison will be done again, and a new `InternalNode` will be created. This new `InternalNode` will point to the `InternalNode` whose `Data` object's value is 15, and its address will be passed back to the `InternalNode` whose `Data` object's value is 3, as shown on line 116.

The net effect is that the new node will be inserted into the list at the right location.

If at all possible, you'll want to step through the insertion of a number of nodes in your debugger. You should be able to watch these methods invoke one another, and the pointers be properly adjusted.

WHAT HAVE YOU LEARNED, DOROTHY?

"If I ever go looking for my heart's desire again, I won't look any further than my own backyard." Although it is true there is no place like home, it is also true that this is nothing like procedural programming. In procedural programming, a controlling method would examine data and invoke functions.

In this, object-oriented approach, each individual object is given a narrow and well-defined set of responsibilities. The linked list is responsible for maintaining the head node. The head node immediately passes the new data on to whatever it points to, without regard to what that might be.

The tail node creates a new node and inserts it whenever it is handed data. It knows only one thing: if this came to me, it gets inserted right before me.

Internal nodes are marginally more complicated; they ask their existing object to compare itself with the new object. Depending on the result, they then either insert or they just pass it along.

Note that the `InternalNode` has no idea how to do the comparison, that is properly left to the object itself. All the `InternalNode` knows is to ask the objects to compare themselves and to expect one of three possible answers. Given one answer, it inserts; otherwise it just passes it along, not knowing or caring where it will end up.

So who's in charge? In a well-designed object-oriented program, no one is in charge. Each object does its own little job, and the net effect is a well-running machine.

In this lesson, you learned to focus on one type of structure, a linked list, that is used to create collections of objects.

LESSON 26
TEMPLATES

In this lesson, you will learn about one of the most exciting and powerful new aspects of ANSI/ISO C++: templates. Templates enable you to build type-safe collections, and you can also use them to improve the linked list considered in the previous lesson.

WHAT ARE TEMPLATES?

The one glaring problem with the linked list considered in the previous lesson was that it knew how to handle only the particular data objects it was created to work with. If you wanted to put anything else into your linked list, you couldn't do it. You couldn't for example, make a linked list of `Car` objects, or of `Cats`, or of any other object that wasn't of the same type as those in the original list.

To solve this problem, you could create a `List` base class and derive from it the `CarList` and `CatsList` classes. You could then cut and paste much of the `LinkedList` class into the new `CatsList` declaration. Next week, when you want to make a list of `Car` objects, you would then have to make a new class, and again you'd cut and paste.

Needless to say, this is not a satisfactory solution. Over time, the `List` class and its derived classes have to be extended. Making sure that all the changes are propagated to all the related classes is a nightmare.

Templates offer a solution to this problem.

PARAMETERIZED TYPES

Templates enable you to teach the compiler how to make a list of any type of thing, rather than creating a set of type-specific lists. A `PartsList` is a list of parts; a `CatList` is a list of cats. The only way in which they differ is the type of the thing on the list. With templates, *the type of the thing on the list becomes a parameter to the definition of the class.*

Instantiation   The act of creating a specific type from a template. The individual classes are called *instances* of the template.

Templates provide you with the ability to create a general class, and pass types as parameters to that class, to build specific instances.

TEMPLATE DEFINITION

You declare a parameterized `List` object (a template for a list) by writing

```
1: template <class T>    // declare the template
2:                       // and the parameter
3: class List            // the class being parameterized
4: {
5:    public:
6:       List();
7:    // full class declaration here
8: };
```

The keyword `template` is used at the beginning of every declaration and definition of a template class. The parameters of the template are after the keyword `template`; they are the items that will change with each instance. For example, in the list template shown in the previous code snippet, the type of the objects stored in the list will change. One instance might store a list of `Integers`, while another might store a list of `Animals`.

In this example, the keyword `class` is used, followed by the identifier `T`. The keyword `class` indicates that this parameter is a type. The identifier `T` is used throughout the rest of the template definition to refer to the parameterized type. One instance of this class will substitute `int` everywhere `T` appears, and another will substitute `Cat`.

To declare an `int` and a `Cat` instance of the parameterized list class, you would write:

```
List<int> anIntList;
List<Cat> aCatList;
```

The object anIntList is of the type list of integers; the object aCatList is of the type ListOfCats. You can now use the type List<int> anywhere you would normally use a type—as the return value from a function, as a parameter to a function, and so forth.

Listing 26.1 parameterizes the List object. This is an excellent technique for building templates: Get your object working on a single type, as you did in the previous lesson. Then parameterize, thereby generalizing your object to handle any type.

LISTING 26.1   DEMONSTRATING PARAMETERIZED LISTS

```
1:    // ************************************************
2:    //    FILE:          Listing 26.1
3:    //
4:    //    PURPOSE:      Demonstrate parameterized list
5:    //    NOTES:
6:    //
7:    //.
8:    //                   All Rights Reserved
9:    //
10:     // object-oriented approach to parameterized
11:     // linked lists. The list delegates to the node.
12:     // The node is an abstract Object type. Three types of
13:     // nodes are used, head nodes, tail nodes and internal
14:     // nodes. Only the internal nodes hold Object.
15:     //
16:     // Created to serve as an object to
17:     // hold in the linked list.
18:     //
19:     // ************************************************
20:
21:
22:     #include <iostream.h>
23:
24:     enum { kIsSmaller, kIsLarger, kIsSame};
25:
26:     // Object class to put into the linked list
27:     // Any class in this linked list must support:
28:     // Show() and Compare()
29:     class Data
30:     {
31:     public:
32:         Data(int val):myValue(val){}
33:         ~Data()
34:         {
```

continues

LISTING 26.1   CONTINUED

```
35:            cout << "Deleting Data object with value: ";
36:            cout << myValue << "\n";
37:        }
38:        int Compare(const Data &) const;
39:        void Show() const { cout << myValue << endl; }
40:    private:
41:        int myValue;
42:    };
43:
44:    // compare is used to decide where in the list
45:    // a particular object belongs.
46:    int Data::Compare(const Data & theOtherObject) const
47:    {
48:        if (myValue < theOtherObject.myValue)
49:            return kIsSmaller;
50:        if (myValue > theOtherObject.myValue)
51:            return kIsLarger;
52:        else
53:            return kIsSame;
54:    }
55:
56:    // Another class to put into the linked list
57:    // Again, every class in this linked list must
➥ support:
58:    // Show and Compare
59:    class Cat
60:    {
61:    public:
62:        Cat(int age): myAge(age){}
63:        ~Cat()
64:        {
65:            cout << "Deleting ";
66:            cout << myAge << " years old Cat.\n";
67:        }
68:        int Compare(const Cat &) const;
69:        void Show() const
70:        {
71:            cout << "This cat is ";
72:            cout << myAge << " years old\n";
73:        }
74:    private:
75:        int myAge;
76:    };
77:
78:
79:    // compare is used to decide where in the list
```

```
80:     // a particular object belongs.
81:     int Cat::Compare(const Cat & theOtherCat) const
82:     {
83:         if (myAge < theOtherCat.myAge)
84:             return kIsSmaller;
85:         if (myAge > theOtherCat.myAge)
86:             return kIsLarger;
87:         else
88:             return kIsSame;
89:     }
90:
91:
92:     // ADT representing the node object in the list
93:     // Every derived class must override Insert and Show
94:     template <class T>
95:     class Node
96:     {
97:     public:
98:         Node(){}
99:         virtual ~Node(){}
100:        virtual Node * Insert(T * theObject)=0;
101:        virtual void Show() const = 0;
102:     private:
103:     };
104:
105:     template <class T>
106:     class InternalNode: public Node<T>
107:     {
108:     public:
109:         InternalNode(T * theObject, Node<T> * next);
110:        virtual ~InternalNode()
110a:          { delete myNext; delete myObject; }
111:        virtual Node<T> * Insert(T * theObject);
112:        virtual void Show() const
113:        {
114:            myObject->Show();
115:            myNext->Show();
116:        }  // delegate!
117:     private:
118:            T * myObject;   // the Object itself
119:            Node<T> * myNext;
120:     };
121:
122:     // All the constructor does is initialize
123:     template <class T>
124:     InternalNode<T>::InternalNode
124a:      (T * theObject, Node<T> * next):
```

continues

LISTING 26.1   CONTINUED

```
125:         myObject(theObject),myNext(next)
126:         {
127:         }
128:
129:         // the meat of the list
130:         // When you put a new object into the list
131:         // it is passed to the node which figures out
132:         // where it goes and inserts it into the list
133:         template <class T>
134:         Node<T> * InternalNode<T>::Insert(T * theObject)
135:         {
136:
137:             // is the new guy bigger or smaller than me?
138:                 int result = myObject->Compare(*theObject);
139:
140:
141:                 switch(result)
142:                 {
143:
144:                 case kIsSame:          // fall through
145:                 case kIsLarger:
146:                     {
147:                         InternalNode<T> * ObjectNode =
148:                         new InternalNode<T>(theObject, this);
149:                         return ObjectNode;
150:                     }
151:
152:
153:                     // node and let HIM handle it.
154:                 case kIsSmaller:
155:                         myNext = myNext->Insert(theObject);
156:                         return this;
157:                 }
158:                 return this;  // appease MSC
159:         }
160:
161:
162:         // Tail node is just a sentinel
163:         template <class T>
164:         class TailNode : public Node<T>
165:         {
166:         public:
167:             TailNode(){}
168:             virtual ~TailNode(){}
169:             virtual Node<T> * Insert(T * theObject);
170:             virtual void Show() const { }
171:
```

```
172:           private:
173:
174:           };
175:
176:           // Must be inserted before me
177:           // as I am the tail and NOTHING comes after me
178:           template <class T>
179:           Node<T> * TailNode<T>::Insert(T * theObject)
180:           {
181:               InternalNode<T> * ObjectNode =
182:                new InternalNode<T>(theObject, this);
183:               return ObjectNode;
184:           }
185:
186:           // Head node has no Object, it just points
187:           // to the very beginning of the list
188:           template <class T>
189:           class HeadNode : public Node<T>
190:           {
191:           public:
192:               HeadNode();
193:               ~HeadNode() { delete myNext; }
194:               virtual Node<T> * Insert(T * theObject);
195:               virtual void Show() { myNext->Show(); }
196:           private:
197:               Node<T> * myNext;
198:           };
199:
200:           // As soon as the head is created
201:           // it creates the tail
202:           template <class T>
203:           HeadNode<T>::HeadNode()
204:           {
205:               myNext = new TailNode<T>;
206:           }
207:
208:           // Nothing comes before the head so just
209:           // pass the Object on to the next node
210:           template <class T>
211:           Node<T> * HeadNode<T>::Insert(T * theObject)
212:           {
213:               myNext = myNext->Insert(theObject);
214:               return this;
215:           }
216:
217:           // I get all the credit and do none of the work
218:       template <class T>
```

continues

LISTING 26.1   CONTINUED

```
219:    class LinkedList
220:        {
221:        public:
222:            LinkedList();
223:            ~LinkedList() { delete myHead; }
224:            void Insert(T * theObject);
225:            void ShowAll() const { myHead->Show(); }
226:        private:
227:            HeadNode<T> * myHead;
228:        };
229:
230:        // At birth, i create the head node
231:        // It creates the tail node
232:        // So an empty list points to the head which
233:        // points to the tail and has nothing between
234:        template <class T>
235:        LinkedList<T>::LinkedList()
236:        {
237:            myHead = new HeadNode<T>;
238:        }
239:
240:        // Delegate, delegate, delegate
241:        template <class T>
242:        void LinkedList<T>::Insert(T * pObject)
243:        {
244:            myHead->Insert(pObject);
245:        }
246:
247:        // test driver program
248:        int main()
249:        {
250:            Cat * pCat;
251:            Data * pData;
252:            int val;
253:            LinkedList<Cat>  ListOfCats;
254:            LinkedList<Data> ListOfData;
255:
256:            // ask the user to produce some values
257:            // put them in the list
258:            for (;;)
259:            {
260:                cout << "What value? (0 to stop): ";
261:                cin >> val;
262:                if (!val)
263:                    break;
264:                pCat = new Cat(val);
```

```
265:                    pData= new Data(val);
266:                    ListOfCats.Insert(pCat);
267:                    ListOfData.Insert(pData);
268:                }
269:
270:                // now walk the list and show the Object
271:                cout << "\n";
272:                ListOfCats.ShowAll();
273:                cout << "\n";
274:                ListOfData.ShowAll();
275:                cout << "\n *********** \n\n";
276:                return 0;
277:            }
```

```
What value? (0 to stop): 5
What value? (0 to stop): 13
What value? (0 to stop): 2
What value? (0 to stop): 9
What value? (0 to stop): 7
What value? (0 to stop): 0

This cat is 2 years old
This cat is 5 years old
This cat is 7 years old
This cat is 9 years old
This cat is 13 years old

2
5
7
9
13

***********

Deleting Data object with value: 13
Deleting Data object with value: 9
Deleting Data object with value: 7
Deleting Data object with value: 5
Deleting Data object with value: 2
Deleting 13 years old Cat.
Deleting 9 years old Cat.
Deleting 7 years old Cat.
Deleting 5 years old Cat.
Deleting 2 years old Cat.
```

OUTPUT

The first thing to notice is the striking similarity to the listing in the previous lesson. The biggest change is that each of the class declarations and methods is prepended with:

```
template class <T>
```

This tells the compiler that you are parameterizing this list on a type that you will define later, when you instantiate the list. For example, the declaration of the Node class now becomes

```
template <class T>
class Node
```

This indicates that Node will not exist as a class in itself, but rather that you will instantiate Nodes of Cats and Nodes of Data objects. The actual type you'll pass in is represented by T.

Thus, InternalNode now becomes InternalNode<T> (read that as "InternalNode of T"). And InternalNode<T> points not to a Data object and another Node; rather, it points to a T (whatever type of object) and a Node<T>. You can see this on lines 118 and 119.

Look carefully at Insert, defined on lines 133–159. The logic is just the same, but where we used to have a specific type (Data) we now have T. Thus, on line 134 the parameter is a pointer to a T. Later, when we instantiate the specific lists, the T will be replaced by the compiler with the right type (Data or Cat).

The important thing is that the InternalNode can continue working, indifferent to the actual type. It knows to ask the objects to compare themselves. It doesn't care whether Cats compare themselves in the same way Data objects do. In fact, we can rewrite this so that Cats don't keep their age; we can have them keep their birth date and compute their relative age on the fly, and the InternalNode won't care a bit.

THE STANDARD TEMPLATE LIBRARY

A new development in C++ is the adoption of the *Standard Template Library* (STL). All the major compiler vendors now offer the STL as part of their compiler. STL is a library of template-based container classes, including vectors, lists, queues, and stacks. The STL also includes a number of common algorithms, including sorting and searching.

The goal of the STL is to give you an alternative to reinventing the wheel for these common requirements. The STL is tested and debugged, offers high performance, and it's free! Most important, the STL is reusable; after you understand how to use an STL container, you can use it in all your programs without reinventing it.

In this lesson, you learned how to use templates to improve the linked list.

LESSON 27
EXCEPTIONS
AND ERROR
HANDLING

In this lesson, you will learn about exceptions and error handling.

HANDLING THE UNEXPECTED

The code you've seen in this book was created for illustration purposes. It has not dealt with errors so that you would not be distracted from the central issues being presented. Real-world programs, on the other hand, must take error conditions into consideration. In fact, in real-world programs, anticipating and handling errors can be the largest part of the code!

You can't eliminate exceptional circumstances; you can only prepare for them. Your users will run out of memory from time to time, and the only question is what you will do.

C++ exception handling provides a type-safe, integrated method for coping with the predictable but unusual conditions that arise while running a program.

EXCEPTIONS

In C++, an *exception* is an object that is passed from the area of code where a problem occurs to the part of the code that is going to handle the problem. The type of the exception determines which area of code will handle the problem, and the contents of the object thrown, if any, it will be used to provide feedback to the user.

The basic idea behind exceptions is fairly straightforward:

- The actual allocation of resources (for example, the allocation of memory or the locking of a file) is usually done at a very low level in the program.

- The logic of what to do when an operation fails, memory cannot be allocated, or a file cannot be locked is usually high in the program, with the code for interacting with the user.

- Exceptions provide an express path from the code that allocates resources to the code that can handle the error condition. If there are intervening layers of functions, they are given an opportunity to clean up memory allocations, but are not required to include code whose only purpose is to pass along the error condition.

HOW EXCEPTIONS ARE USED

 A try block   A set of statements that begins with the word try, is followed by an opening brace, and ends with a closing brace.

For example

```
try
{
Function();
};
```

try blocks are created to surround areas of code that may have a problem. For example

```
try
{
SomeDangerousFunction();
}
```

catch blocks handle the exceptions thrown in the try block. For example:

```
try
{
```

```
SomeDangerousFunction();
}
catch(OutOfMemory)
{
// take some actions
}
catch(FileNotFound)
{
// take other action
}
```

The basic steps in using exceptions are:

1. Identify those areas of the program in which you begin an operation that might raise an exception, and put them in try blocks.

2. Create catch blocks to catch the exceptions if they are thrown, to clean up allocated memory, and to inform the user as appropriate. Listing 27.1 illustrates the use of both try blocks and catch blocks.

Exceptions are objects used to transmit information about a problem.

A try block is a block, surrounded by braces, in which an exception may be thrown.

A catch block is the block immediately following a try block, in which exceptions are handled.

When an exception is thrown (or raised), control transfers to the catch block immediately following the current try block.

LISTING 27.1   RAISING AN EXCEPTION

```
0:        #include <iostream.h>
1:
2:        const int DefaultSize = 10;
3:
4:        // define the exception class
5:        class xBoundary
6:        {
7:        public:
8:            xBoundary() {}
9:            ~xBoundary() {}
```

```
10:     private:
11:     };
12:
13:
14:     class Array
15:     {
16:     public:
17:         // constructors
18:         Array(int itsSize = DefaultSize);
19:         Array(const Array &rhs);
20:         ~Array() { delete [] pType;}
21:
22:         // operators
23:         Array& operator=(const Array&);
24:         int& operator[](int offSet);
25:         const int& operator[](int offSet) const;
26:
27:         // accessors
28:         int GetitsSize() const { return itsSize; }
29:
30:         // friend function
31:        friend ostream& operator<<
31a:           (ostream&, const Array&);
32:
33:     private:
34:         int *pType;
35:         int  itsSize;
36:     };
37:
38:
39:     Array::Array(int size):
40:     itsSize(size)
41:     {
42:         pType = new int[size];
43:         for (int i = 0; i<size; i++)
44:             pType[i] = 0;
45:     }
46:
47:
48:     Array& Array::operator=(const Array &rhs)
49:     {
50:         if (this == &rhs)
51:             return *this;
52:         delete [] pType;
53:         itsSize = rhs.GetitsSize();
54:         pType = new int[itsSize];
```

continues

LISTING 27.1   CONTINUED

```
55:            for (int i = 0; i<itsSize; i++)
56:                pType[i] = rhs[i];
57:            return *this;
58:        }
59:
60:        Array::Array(const Array &rhs)
61:        {
62:            itsSize = rhs.GetitsSize();
63:            pType = new int[itsSize];
64:            for (int i = 0; i<itsSize; i++)
65:                pType[i] = rhs[i];
66:        }
67:
68:
69:        int& Array::operator[](int offSet)
70:        {
71:            int size = GetitsSize();
72:            if (offSet >= 0 && offSet < GetitsSize())
73:                return pType[offSet];
74:            throw xBoundary();
75:            return pType[offSet]; // to appease MSC!
76:
77:        }
78:
79:
80:        const int& Array::operator[](int offSet) const
81:        {
82:            int mysize = GetitsSize();
83:            if (offSet >= 0 && offSet < GetitsSize())
84:                return pType[offSet];
85:            throw xBoundary();
86:            return pType[offSet]; // to appease MSC!
87:        }
88:
89:        ostream& operator<<
89a:         (ostream& output, const Array& theArray)
90:        {
91:            for (int i = 0; i<theArray.GetitsSize(); i++)
92:            {
92a:                output << "[" << i << "] ";
92b                output << theArray[i] << endl;
92c:            }
93:            return output;
94:        }
95:
```

```
96:        int main()
97:        {
98:            Array intArray(20);
99:            try
100:            {
101:                for (int j = 0; j< 100; j++)
102:                {
103:                    intArray[j] = j;
104:                    cout << "intArray[" ;
104a:                   cout << j << "] okay..." << endl;
105:                }
106:            }
107:            catch (xBoundary)
108:            {
109:                cout << "Unable to process your input!\n";
110:            }
111:            cout << "Done.\n";
112:            return 0;
113:        }
```

OUTPUT

```
intArray[0] okay...
intArray[1] okay...
intArray[2] okay...
intArray[3] okay...
intArray[4] okay...
intArray[5] okay...
intArray[6] okay...
intArray[7] okay...
intArray[8] okay...
intArray[9] okay...
intArray[10] okay...
intArray[11] okay...
intArray[12] okay...
intArray[13] okay...
intArray[14] okay...
intArray[15] okay...
intArray[16] okay...
intArray[17] okay...
intArray[18] okay...
intArray[19] okay...
Unable to process your input!
Done.
```

Listing 27.1 presents a somewhat stripped-down Array class, created just
to illustrate this simple use of exceptions. On lines 5–11, a very simple
exception class is declared, xBoundary. The most important thing to notice

about this class is that there is absolutely nothing that makes it an exception class. In fact, any class, with any name and any number of methods and variables, will do just fine as an exception. What makes this an exception is only that it is *thrown*, as shown on line 74, and that it is caught, as shown on line 107!

The offset operators throw xBoundary when the client of the class attempts to access data outside the array. This is far superior to the way normal arrays handle such a request; they just return whatever garbage happens to be in memory at that location, a sure-fire way to crash your program.

On line 99, the keyword try begins a try block that ends on line 106. Within that try block, 100 integers are added to the array that was declared on line 98.

On line 107, the catch block to catch xBoundary exceptions is declared.

A catch block   A series of statements, each of which begins with the word catch, followed by an exception type in parentheses, followed by an opening brace, and ending with a closing brace.

For example

```
Try
{
Function();
};
Catch (OutOfMemory)
{
// take action
}
```

USING try BLOCKS AND catch BLOCKS

Figuring out where to put your try blocks is probably the hardest part of using exceptions; it is not always obvious which actions might raise an exception. The next question is where to catch the exception. It may be that you'll want to throw all memory exceptions where the memory is allocated, but you'll want to catch the exceptions high in the program, where you deal with the user interface.

When trying to determine try block locations, look at where you allocate memory or use resources. Other things to look for are out-of-bounds errors, illegal input, and so forth.

CATCHING EXCEPTIONS

Here's how catching exceptions works: When an exception is thrown, the call stack is examined. The *call stack* is the list of function calls created when one part of the program invokes another function.

The call stack tracks the execution path. If main() calls the function Animal::GetFavoriteFood(), and GetFavoriteFood() calls Animal::LookupPreferences(), which in turn calls fstream::operator>>(), all of these are on the call stack. A recursive function might be on the call stack many times.

The exception is passed up the call stack to each enclosing block. As the stack is unwound, the destructors for local objects on the stack are invoked, and the objects are destroyed.

After each try block are one or more catch statements. If the exception matches one of the catch statements, it is considered to be handled by having that statement execute. If it doesn't match any, the unwinding of the stack continues.

If the exception reaches all the way to the beginning of the program (main()) and is still not caught, a built-in handler is called that terminates the program.

It is important to note that the exception unwinding of the stack is a one-way street. As it progresses, the stack is unwound, and objects on the stack are destroyed. There is no going back: Once the exception is handled, the program continues after the try block of the catch statement that handled the exception.

Thus, in Listing 27.1, execution will continue on line 111, the first line after the try block of the catch statement that handled the xBoundary exception. Remember that when an exception is raised, program flow continues after the catch block, not after the point where the exception was thrown.

MORE THAN ONE catch SPECIFICATION

It is possible for more than one condition to cause an exception. In this case, the catch statements can be lined up one after another, much like the conditions in a switch statement. The equivalent to the default statement is the "catch everything" statement, indicated by catch(...).

CATCHING BY REFERENCE AND POLYMORPHISM

You can take advantage of the fact that exceptions are just classes to use them polymorphically. By passing the exception by reference, you can use the inheritance hierarchy to take the appropriate action based on the runtime type of the exception. Listing 27.2 illustrates using exceptions polymorphically.

LISTING 27.2   POLYMORPHIC EXCEPTIONS

```
0:      #include <iostream.h>
1:
2:      const int DefaultSize = 10;
3:
4:      // define the exception classes
5:          class xBoundary {};
6:
7:          class xSize
8:          {
9:          public:
10:             xSize(int size):itsSize(size) {}
11:             virtual ~xSize(){}
12:             virtual int GetSize() const { return itsSize; }
13:             virtual void PrintError() const
14:             {
14a:                cout << "Size error. Received: ";
14b:                cout  << itsSize << endl; }
14c:             }
15:          protected:
16:             int itsSize;
17:          };
18:
```

```
19:        class xTooBig : public xSize
20:        {
21:        public:
22:            xTooBig(int size):xSize(size){}
23:            virtual void PrintError() const
24:              { cout << "Too big! Received: ";
25:                cout << xSize::itsSize << endl; }
26:        };
27:
28:        class xTooSmall : public xSize
29:        {
30:        public:
31:            xTooSmall(int size):xSize(size){}
32:            virtual void PrintError() const
33:              { cout << "Too small! Received: ";
34:                cout << xSize::itsSize << endl; }
35:        };
36:
37:        class xZero   : public xTooSmall
38:        {
39:        public:
40:            xZero(int size):xTooSmall(size){}
41:            virtual void PrintError() const
42:              { cout << "Zero!!. Received: ";
43:                cout << xSize::itsSize << endl; }
44:        };
45:
46:        class xNegative : public xSize
47:        {
48:        public:
49:            xNegative(int size):xSize(size){}
50:            virtual void PrintError() const
51:              { cout << "Negative! Received: ";
52:                cout << xSize::itsSize << endl; }
53:        };
54:
55:
56:     class Array
57:     {
58:     public:
59:        // constructors
60:        Array(int itsSize = DefaultSize);
61:        Array(const Array &rhs);
62:        ~Array() { delete [] pType;}
63:
64:        // operators
65:        Array& operator=(const Array&);
```

continues

LISTING 27.2   CONTINUED

```
66:          int& operator[](int offSet);
67:          const int& operator[](int offSet) const;
68:
69:          // accessors
70:          int GetitsSize() const { return itsSize; }
71:
72:          // friend function
73:       friend ostream& operator<<
73a:          (ostream&, const Array&);
74:
75:
76:     private:
77:         int *pType;
78:         int  itsSize;
79:     };
80:
81:     Array::Array(int size):
82:     itsSize(size)
83:     {
84:        if (size == 0)
85:           throw xZero(size);
86:
87:        if (size < 0)
88:           throw xNegative(size);
89:
90:        if (size < 10)
91:           throw xTooSmall(size);
92:
93:        if (size > 30000)
94:           throw xTooBig(size);
95:
96:
97:        pType = new int[size];
98:        for (int i = 0; i<size; i++)
99:           pType[i] = 0;
100:    }
101:
102:    int& Array::operator[] (int offset)
103:    {
104:        int size = GetitsSize();
105:        if (offset >= 0 && offset < GetitsSize())
106:           return pType[offset];
107:        throw xBoundary();
```

```
108:              return pType[offset];
109:      }
110:
111:      const int& Array::operator[] (int offset) const
112:      {
113:          int size = GetitsSize();
114:          if (offset >= 0 && offset < GetitsSize())
115:            return pType[offset];
116:          throw xBoundary();
117:            return pType[offset];
118:      }
119:
120:      int main()
121:      {
122:
123:          try
124:          {
125:              int choice;
126:              cout << "Enter the array size: ";
127:              cin >> choice;
128:              Array intArray(choice);
129:              for (int j = 0; j< 100; j++)
130:              {
131:                  intArray[j] = j;
132:                  cout << "intArray[";
132a:                 cout << j << "] okay..." << endl;
133:              }
134:          }
135:          catch (xBoundary)
136:          {
137:              cout << "Unable to process your input!\n";
138:          }
139:          catch (xSize& theException)
140:          {
141:              theException.PrintError();
142:          }
143:          catch (...)
144:          {
145:              cout << "Something went wrong,";
145a:             cout << " but I've no idea what!" << endl;
146:          }
147:          cout << "Done.\n";
148:        return 0;
149:      }
```

OUTPUT

```
Enter the array size: 5
Too small! Received: 5
Done.

Enter the array size: 50000
Too big! Received: 50000
Done.

Enter the array size: 12
intArray[0] okay...
intArray[1] okay...
intArray[2] okay...
intArray[3] okay...
intArray[4] okay...
intArray[5] okay...
intArray[6] okay...
intArray[7] okay...
intArray[8] okay...
intArray[9] okay...
intArray[10] okay...
intArray[11] okay...
Unable to process your input!
Done.
Press any key to continue
```

Listing 27.2 declares a virtual method in the xSize class, PrintError(), that prints an error message and the actual size of the class. This is overridden in each of the derived classes.

On line 139, the exception object is declared to be a reference. When PrintError() is called with a reference to an object, polymorphism causes the correct version of PrintError() to be invoked. The first time through we ask for an array of size 5. This causes the TooSmall exception to be thrown; that is the xSize exception caught on line 139. The second time through we ask for an array of 50,000 and that causes the TooBig exception to be thrown. This is also caught on line 139, but polymorphism causes the right error string to print. When we finally ask for an array of size 12, the array is populated until the xBoundary exception is thrown and caught on line 135.

In this lesson, you learned how to work with exceptions.

LESSON 28
NEXT STEPS

In this lesson, you will learn how to keep on learning C++.

WHERE TO GET HELP AND ADVICE

You now know the fundamentals of C++, but this is the beginning, not the end of your study. If you have discovered that you enjoy programming in C++, you may want to consider reading either a more in-depth primer (such as my book *Teach Yourself C++ In 21 Days*, Third Edition) or perhaps an advanced text on C++ (such as my book *C++ Unleashed*).

Another very important thing you will want to do as a C++ programmer is to tap into one or another C++ conference on an online service. These groups supply immediate contact with hundreds or thousands of C++ programmers who can answer your questions, offer advice, and provide a sounding board for your ideas.

I participate in the C++ Internet newsgroups (`comp.lang.c++` and `comp.lang.c++.moderated`), and I recommend them as excellent sources of information and support, and you may find that helping others works wonders to clarify your own thinking.

Also, you may want to look for local user groups. Many cities have C++ interest groups where you can meet other programmers and exchange ideas.

MAGAZINES

There is one more thing you can do to strengthen your skills: subscribe to a good magazine on C++ programming. The absolute best magazine of this kind, I believe, is C++ Report from SIGS Publications. Every issue is packed with useful articles. Save them; what you don't care about today will become critically important tomorrow. (Caveat: I have a monthly column in C++ Report—and thus a conflict of interest. That said, I still believe it is a terrific publication).

You can reach C++ Report (http://www.creport.com/) at SIGS
Publications, P.O. Box 2031, Langhorne, PA 19047-9700.

STAYING IN TOUCH

If you have comments, suggestions, or ideas about this book or other
books, I'd love to hear them. Please write to me at jliberty@
libertyassociates.com, or check out my Web site: www.libertyassoci-
ates.com where I provide support for my book and host an email list for
my readers. I look forward to hearing from you.

APPENDIX A

OPERATOR PRECEDENCE

It is important to understand that operators have a precedence, but it is not essential to memorize the precedence.

Precedence is the order in which a program performs the operations in a formula. If one operator has precedence over another operator, it is evaluated first.

Higher precedence operators "bind tighter" than lower precedence operators; thus, higher precedence operators are evaluated first. The lower the rank in the following chart, the higher the precedence.

TABLE A.1 OPERATOR PRECEDENCE

RANK	NAME	OPERATOR
1	scope resolution	::
2	member selection, subscripting,	. ->
	function calls, postfix increment	()
	and decrement	++ --
3	sizeof, prefix increment and decrement,	++ --
	complement, and, not, unary minus and plus,	^ !
	address of and dereference, new, new[], delete,	- +
	delete[], casting, sizeof()	& *
		()
4	member selection for pointer	.* ->*
5	multiply, divide, modulo	* / %
6	add, subtract	+ -

continues

TABLE A.1   CONTINUED

RANK	NAME	OPERATOR
7	shift	<< >>
8	inequality relational	< <= > >=
9	equality, inequality	== !=
10	bitwise AND	&
11	bitwise exclusive OR	^
12	bitwise OR	I
13	logical AND	&&
14	logical OR	II
15	conditional	?:
16	assignment operators	= *= /= %=
		+= -= <<= >>=
		&= I= ^=
17	throw operator	throw
18	comma	,

INDEX

reassigning, 100-101
returning
multiple values with, 109-110
nonexistent objects, 117-119
objects on heap, 119-121
registers, 85
relational operators, 31-32
relationships
is-a, 180
nodes (establishing), 201
resources
allocating, 219
magazines, 231-232
newsgroups, 231
responsibility, delegating, 195, 202, 205
restoring memory (free store), 87
retrieving values, 14. *See also* variables
return statements, 12, 44
return types (header), 12
return values, 44-45, 87
returning
addresses, 203
functions, 11-12
main( ) function (int), 11
memory (free store), 87
multiple values, 107-110
objects by value, 111-112
references, 117-121
values, 10-12

S

semicolon (;), 23-24
shallow copies (objects), 125
short int, 16-18
short integers, 16
signatures, 12
signed integers, 17
signed types, 16
singly linked lists, 194
size (integers/types/variables), 16-17
slash (/), 26
slash-star comment (/*), 11
source code files (.cpp), creating, 5
stack, 85-86
Standard C++, 3
standard output, 3
Standard Template Library
(STL), 216-217
starting projects, 4-5. *See also* statements
statements, 12, 23-25, 77. *See also* commands; expressions
#define (defining constants), 21

assignment, 23
break statements, 68, 71-72, 78
case, 78
catch, 225-226
catch blocks, 224
catch(...) (catch everything), 226
compound, 24
const (defining constants), 21
continue, 71-72
cout, 10
default, 78, 226
executing, 225
functions, 42
if, 33-36
null (for loops), 73
return, 12, 44
simple, 23
switch, 77-79, 226
try blocks, 219
whitespace, 23-24
STL (Standard Template Library),
216-217
storage locations, 19. *See also* constants
storing
addresses, 81, 85
data (free store), 85
lists, 208
objects, 193
values (variable types), 14, 17. *See
also* variables
stray pointers, 97
strcpy( ) function, 160-161
String class, 162
strings, 158-160
copying, 160-162
syntax, 159
terminating, 158
strncpy( ) function, 161-162
swap( ) function, 44
switch statements, 77-79, 226
symbolic constants, 19-20
syntax (enumerated constants), 21

T

tabs (Projects), 5
tail nodes, 193-195, 201, 205
template keyword, 208
templates, 207-209
building, 209
creating types, 208-209
declaring, 208